I CHING COIN PREDICTION

By Da Liu

T'ai Chi Ch'uan and I Ching
The Taoist Health Exercise Book
I Ching Coin Prediction

I CHING
COIN
PREDICTION

Da Liu

HARPER & ROW, PUBLISHERS
New York, Evanston, San Francisco, London

FIRST EDITION

Designed by Patricia Dunbar

Library of Congress Cataloging in Publication Data

Liu, Da.
    I ching coin prediction.
    Includes an English translation of the text of the
I ching.
    1. Divination. 2. I ching. I. Title.
II. I ching. English. 1975.
BF1770.C5L58   133.3'3   73-18695
ISBN 0-06-061664-9
ISBN 0-06-061665-6 (pbk.)

Contents

Preface

As long as there has been a China, the *I Ching* has helped to guide it, through prophecy and philosophy. China's oldest history book, the *Shu Ching*, records that ancient governments, when considering an important undertaking, placed their ultimate trust in prophecy—above the judgment of even the emperor. The great Chinese sage Confucius, in his work *Ch'un Ch'iu*, or "Spring and Autumn," describes how dukes consulted oracles for advice on wars, marriages, and the future of newborn princes. In the Shang-Yin Dynasty (1766–1154 B.C.), even the names emperors chose for themselves were related to the Five Elements, which were then and are now important in Chinese prophecy. In the T'ang Dynasty (A.D. 618–935), a list of predictions using the *I Ching* was compiled at the request of the emperor, and this list, called *T'uei Pei T'u*, or "Great Prophecy," still has great influence among Chinese people all over the world.

This aspect of Chinese history has always enthralled me. From reading tales of the past as a boy, I became fascinated by the great statesmen, philosophers, and sages who predicted the future. Those specializing in military strategy, called Teachers of the Army, detected the situation and strategy of the enemy while devising tactics of their own; those called National Teachers were consulted by kings and governments (especially after astrological changes had occurred) on how to avoid war, famine, and other disasters. There were also those who, though not in official positions, made their living by telling people how to get good fortune and avoid misfortune in the future. Every generation had these seers, and what they knew best were the *I Ching* methods of prediction. Many stories exist both in historical record and in oral tradition about the strategists, prophets, and philosophers, and of their amazing accuracy. As I grew—in Peking, Shanghai, and Nanking—so did my fascination. I began to study the *I Ching* and to learn the arts of prediction from elders, even fortunetellers. (Many times my parents reproached me: "Do you want to be a fortuneteller?")

During the Sino-Japanese War, I continued to study the *I Ching* and related books and to consult people concerned with prediction, including monks, hermits, and fortunetellers. I began to make predictions for myself and others. I made a series of predictions about the outcome of the Japanese war, and then about the future of Nationalist and Communist China, all of which have proven to be remarkably correct. My study of *I Ching* prediction continued following my emigration to the United States. Even now I write down in the first page of my diary the future of the coming year: the events for every month, even every week. Then at the end of each month and year I check my predictions. They have been strikingly accurate.

For the average person, the idea behind consulting the *I Ching* is to receive an indication of coming good fortune or misfortune. Then one may act or not act accordingly. It is much like hearing a weather forecast: you cannot change the weather, but if you know it is going to rain, you can avoid much discomfort. And if you find that a storm is coming, you can anchor your boat in the harbor. Of course, predictions can also be positive: if you know when it will rain, you can plant your seed at the proper time.

Even after the arrival of good fortune or misfortune, the philosophy of life contained in the *I Ching* may be consulted for guidance. If good fortune is yours, you should keep your present manner and avoid lapsing into arrogance or carelessness; otherwise the situation may slip into misfortune. If misfortune is your fate, repentance and humility may gain you good fortune. Thus fortune, like the weather, changes according to the conditions around it: if it is sunny and also cold and dry, it will remain sunny; and if it is raining but windy, the winds will disperse the clouds and it will become sunny once more. The *I Ching* says: "Therefore the superior man contemplates these images in times of rest and meditates on the judgments. When he undertakes something, he contemplates the changes and ponders on the oracles. Therefore he is blessed by heaven. 'Good fortune.' " And Confucius wrote that if he could add more years to his life, he would give fifty to the study of the *I Ching*, so that he might be without great faults.

Although the *I Ching* has been revered in the East for over three thousand years as a holy book, in the West it is not nearly so well known. In recent years, however, there has been a surging discovery of this remarkable book. In 1950 Richard Wilhelm's classic German version appeared in an English translation,* including a lengthy foreword by the eminent Swiss psychiatrist C. G. Jung. Jung wrote not only of the book's philosophy but also of its use in predicting the future; in fact, much of his essay relates how he consulted the *I Ching* about whether or not to write that foreword! In his auto-biography, Jung wrote further of his experiences with the *I Ching*—how he would sit under an old pear tree for hours, asking it questions. He was so impressed by the book that he once advised a friend always to obey it, for it never made mistakes. The German author Herman Hesse also plunged deeply into the wisdom of the *I Ching*. In his last novel, *The Glass Bead Game*, there are two scenes in which his characters consult the *I Ching* for prediction. Indeed, Hesse once said that the *I Ching* can transform a life.

In spite of the increased interest in *I Ching* prediction, there has yet to be a book specifically on this subject. This version primarily hopes to satisfy the reader who is interested in the coin method of prediction. I have two main goals: to give a more detailed explanation of lines, trigrams, and hexagrams for prediction purposes; and to explain the coin method, which does not require the numerical calculations of other techniques. Thus the reader can save time and avoid ambiguity, using this book as a guide to interpret the answers he receives to his questions. For those readers who are interested in using yarrow stalks for prediction, I have also included an explanation of that method.

I am deeply grateful to the many people who helped me in the preparation of this book, including Robert A. Anderson, Susan Delone, Ann Himler, Janice Kovar, Maureen Owen, and Olive Wong.

The *I Ching* contains every reality in the world; it knows no limits of time or place. One need only ask the truth of it, and it will resound with wisdom. "The Changes are what has enabled the holy sages to reach all depths and to grasp the seeds of all things."

DA LIU

New York City

* In this Preface and in the Introduction I quote the *I Ching* from Cary F. Baynes's English translation of the Wilhelm version: *The I Ching: or Book of Changes* (Princeton: Princeton University Press, 1950 and 1967). In the remainder of the book the translation of the *I Ching* is my own.

I CHING COIN PREDICTION

Introduction

Background of the *I Ching*

The *I Ching*, or "Book of Changes," is the root of Chinese civilization. Its original form was devised by Fu Shi, a legendary Chinese sage who lived during the age of hunting and fishing over 4,500 years ago. First he invented the unbroken and broken lines to represent the polar forces of the universe: positive (*yang*) and negative (*yin*). Then, from his direct observation of the world—the earth and sky, birds and animals, and himself—he constructed the eight trigrams, each of which consists of three lines and stands for some aspect of nature, society, and the individual person. Thus the *I Ching* is grounded in nature and the everyday world, not in abstruse metaphysics.

In 1150 B.C., King Wen, the progenitor of the Chou Dynasty (1150–249 B.C.), assembled the original version of what we know today as the *I Ching*. While he was being held captive for seven years by the emperor Shin Chou (who feared his popularity), King Wen arranged and named the sixty-four hexagrams—each consisting of six lines— and wrote a commentary for each known as "The Judgment." After King Wen's death his son, the Duke of Chou, completed his work by adding commentaries on the individual lines of the hexagrams as well as a commentary on each Judgment. These commentaries provided the philosophical framework for *I Ching* prediction.

Five hundred years later Confucius came in contact with the Book of Changes. So impressed was he that he three times wore out the leather thongs which bound his copy! Not only did he study it extensively, but he and his disciples also wrote a series of essays known as the "Ten Wings," which came to be considered part of the *I Ching* itself. The Ten Wings may be compared to a lengthy book review, in

1

which Confucius explains and analyzes the philosophical and spiritual bases of the work. They include a discussion of the attributes of the eight trigrams, a commentary on the Symbols, and miscellaneous notes on the hexagrams.

After Confucius, many scholars and philosophers studied the *I Ching* and contributed commentaries, especially in the Han Dynasty (206 B.C.–A.D. 205), when much was written on prediction. The *I Ching* was one of the few books spared in the great book burning of 213 B.C., in which the emperor Chin Shih Hwang Ti destroyed all books not relating to medicine, agriculture, or divination. The *I Ching* has always been considered a sacred book in China, and generations of scholars, rulers, and military strategists have consulted it before making decisions.

Hexagrams, Lines, Trigrams

In his foreword to Richard Wilhelm's version of the *I Ching*, C. G. Jung wrote, "For more than thirty years I have interested myself in this oracle technique, or method of exploring the unconscious, for it has seemed to me of uncommon significance." The *I Ching* is an investigation of the unconscious—*not* of superstition. The *I Ching* itself says: "Therefore the superior man, whenever he has to make or do something, consults the Changes, and he does so in words. It takes up his communications like an echo; neither far nor near, neither dark nor deep exist for it, and thus he learns of the things of the future."

This exploration is highly systematized. The *I Ching* is like a catalogue containing sixty-four categories: the hexagrams. Each hexagram is made up of six broken or unbroken lines. Accompanying and commenting upon the hexagrams are the Judgment and the Symbol, which apply to and contain ideas from nature, society, and the individual. For the person who consults them, the hexagrams provide knowledge, wisdom, virtue, and also warning, advice, and caution.

For example, Hexagram 3, *Chun,* Difficulty in the Beginning, indicates, as its name implies, that everything is difficult at its inception; therefore one should prepare and have patience. In nature this is the interval between spring and winter, when the weather is still cold but plants are preparing under the ground to sprout. They must have enough energy to break through the frozen ground and, once they come out, to suffer the unfavorable weather. Thus when a person has a new commitment or undertaking, he should be well prepared and have the patience to deal with the initial difficulties which society will offer. In the Symbol for this hexagram, the first sentence indicates the natural difficulties referred to by the hexagram: "Clouds and thunder symbolize Difficulty in the Beginning." The second sentence shows the relation of this situation to the individual person and society: "The superior man makes order out of disorder."

The next hexagram, number 4, in its reference to nature depicts the growth of plants and trees; in terms of the individual, it indicates a person growing up, as shown by its name, *Meng*, or Youth. But plants and youth should both get good nourishment (or good education), so Hexagram 5 is Nourishment, or Waiting. In nature, weeds compete with crops for nourishment; in the world, nations and people struggle for natural resources; and in society, businessmen compete for jobs. Even children sometimes fight. So the next hexagram, 6, is Conflict, and the one after that is the result of conflict: the Army, *Shih*.

The sequence of later hexagrams indicates misfortune hiding in good fortune, or vice versa. Hexagram 11, *T'ai*, Peace, signifies good fortune or favorable conditions, but following it is *Pi*, Stagnation. Hexagram 23, *Po*, Decay, is also a bad situation, but the next hexagram is *Fu*, Return, which indicates good fortune again.

Other hexagrams show a succession of favorable conditions. Number 13 is *T'ung Jen*, Fellowship of Men, a condition in which persons facing danger or difficulty join together to coordinate their efforts, to work or to fight. The next hexagram, *Ta Yu*, Great Possessions, means that through their struggle the people have become prosperous again. But if they now become arrogant or lazy, misfortune will be the result; the following hexagram, 15, Modesty, shows the attitude which a person must have to maintain his good fortune. With modesty, he attains favor everywhere. Unlike other hexagrams that depict favorable situations, in 15 every line is fortunate. (Even *T'ai*, Peace, has a top line of misfortune). So the next hexagram, *Yu* is Happiness.

Like the hexagrams they make up, most of the six lines can be interpreted as having three elements: a Symbol, an Event, and a Judgment. Lines in hexagrams are numbered from the bottom up. For the fifth line of Hexagram 11, *T'ai*, Peace, "Six in the fifth place" is the

Symbol, indicating that the line is a broken line and fifth from the bottom of the hexagram. The Event is "The Emperor I gives his daughter in marriage." "This will bring blessings and great good fortune" is the Judgment, which points to a bright future for the predictor in his present situation. The Event of this line refers to a particular emperor, which, incidentally, is not infrequent: in Hexagram 36, *Ming I*, every line refers to a specific person.

The six lines reflect the stages of growth or the sequence of events within an individual hexagram. In the first hexagram, *Ch'ien*, the Creative, the bottom line reads, "The hibernating dragon does not act." The beginning of this hexagram thus signifies something in an immature state—an idea in the mind that has not yet led to action or commitment, or a child still incapable of contributing to society. The second line says, "The dragon is seen on the field." The scene or event is now beginning; the child is growing up and starting to interact with society. The second line continues, "There is benefit in meeting a great man," meaning that it is time for the child to have a teacher. The third line refers to that period of transition from attending school to living in society: "The superior man works creatively the whole day, and is cautious in the evening." One is still studying, but he is about to graduate and thinking hard about what to do with his life. In the fourth line the dragon "leaps from the abyss"; this is the great jump from home and school into society. By the fifth line the person has matured and holds a high and powerful position: "The dragon flies in the heavens." But the last line indicates that after a time, he will be retired or his business closed: "The dragon is arrogant and will have cause to repent."

In other hexagrams, although the overall situation may be favorable or unfavorable, any of the six individual lines may indicate a departure from the general conditions—just as in the warmest of summers some days are cool and pleasant, and in wintertime there are days that are warm. One of the lessons to be learned from the sequence of conditions in both the lines and the hexagrams is that one should not be discouraged by misfortune, nor become haughty or careless after meeting good fortune. This teaching can be found in Confucius's *Ta Chuan*, the Great Treatise of the *I Ching*.

The same line may contain both good fortune and misfortune. In number 13, *T'ung Jen*, Fellowship of Men, the fifth line reads, "They cry and lament. Later they laugh." And in Hexagram 56, *Lu*, the Exile, the sixth line reads, "The exile laughs in the beginning, laments later." In many places in the *I Ching* it is of benefit to continue or persist in what one is doing; in other places to persist is imprudent. In Hexagram 60, *Chieh*, Limitation, the first line advises that if one "does not go out of the door and courtyard" (if he maintains his present position), there will be no blame; while the second line predicts misfortune for the same action.

In addition to the individual lines and the hexagrams as a whole, a person consulting the *I Ching* should consider the eight three-lined trigrams. Four trigrams are found in each hexagram. The trigram has an Attribute, Symbol, and Characteristic, and is related to the Five Elements (also called the Five States of Change): wood, fire, earth, metal, water. At some point in the history of prediction the trigrams also became associated with the astrological symbols—the twelve signs of the zodiac.

The hexagram is composed of two primary trigrams, the upper and the lower (Fig. 1). The upper (lines four, five, and six) is considered

The Four Trigrams of a Hexagram

Primary Trigrams: Nuclear Trigrams:

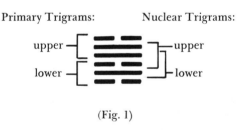

upper   upper

lower   lower

(Fig. 1)

to be outside and above, the lower (lines one, two, and three) to be inside and below. Also in the hexagram are the two nuclear trigrams (Fig. 1). The second, third, and fourth lines constitute the lower nuclear trigram, and the third, fourth, and fifth lines the upper. Since ancient times the nuclear trigrams have been used in prediction. They provide us with more detail and enable us to be more precise in judging good fortune and misfortune in the future, answering the questions how, why, who, when, where, and how much.

To illustrate how to interpret a hexagram by using the trigrams, let us look at Hexagram 42, *I*, Increase, which, according to the *Ta Chuan*, signifies the history of civilization. The upper and lower primary trigrams are both related to wood, one of the Five Elements.

The upper is soft wood, the lower is hard wood. The upper trigram, *Sun*, also means penetration; the lower, *Chen*, means movement. The lower nuclear trigram, *K'un*, means soil or land, and the upper nuclear trigram, *Ken*, means mountain or highland. Both nuclear trigrams relate to the earth, another of the Five Elements. So the hexagram as a whole indicates a wooden instrument penetrating the soil and being moved; tilling the soil. Thus civilization began.

Coins and Prediction

In the *Ta Chuan*, Confucius writes "The Changes have no consciousness, no action; they are quiescent and do not move. But if they are stimulated, they penetrate all situations under heaven." "Stimulating" the Changes means using instruments of prediction to determine the hexagram that contains the answer to your question.

In Chinese prediction there are two main systems: symbolic and numerical. This differentiation began in ancient times when tortoise shells and their markings were associated with symbols, and yarrow stalks with their accompanying calculations with numbers. Among the various instruments used to consult the oracles, these two were the most important and the most popular. It is believed that in the Shang-Yin Dynasty animal bones and tortoise shells were used because the people were not far removed from a hunting and fishing culture. As the culture developed into an agricultural one during the Chou Dynasty, bones and shells were replaced by plants. In the *I Ching*, yarrow stalks are frequently mentioned and designated as an integral part of its use: "In ancient times the holy sages made the Book of Changes thus: They invented the yarrow-stalk oracle to lend aid in a mysterious way to the light of the gods."

The use of yarrow stalks, however, was time-consuming and required eighteen separate hand manipulations, making it too complicated for general use and acceptance. During the time of the Warring States (403–221 B.C.), therefore, coins were introduced as an instrument of prediction.

The Warring-States period began almost eighty years after the death of Confucius. This was the last part of the Chou Dynasty, and, as its name implies, a period of incessant fighting. Large states were constantly annexing smaller ones, and dukes were usurping both kings and each other. But "war is both a poison and a medicine."

Just as there was great competition between the states, so there was rivalry within them as scholars and experts vied for official positions. This led to a great many advancements in society, especially in the field of military strategy.

In the field of prediction as well there was an impetus for new development: with so much strife and uncertainty people had a greater need to predict events, and to predict them faster. It was in this period that the great philosopher and military strategist Kuei Kuo Tse lived. A Taoist who led a hermit's life in the mountains and was regarded as a mysterious sage, he studied the *I Ching* deeply and contemplated how the yin-and-yang principle applied to everything in the world, both physical and spiritual. Hundreds of statesmen, military strategists, magicians, and astrologers studied under him and left to serve in various states as high officials and officers. From his study of military strategy and then prediction, Kuei Kuo Tse came to feel that using the yarrow stalks was too time-consuming and not suitable for the turbulent society of his day. So he devised the use of coins for prediction to replace both yarrow stalks and tortoise shells.

The coin method became widely used in Chinese society, but the number of coins used varied. Sometimes only one coin was used to obtain a simple yes/no or good/bad answer, sometimes five, six, or even ten coins were employed. In the later Han Dynasty, the premier of Shou Kingdom was Chu Go Liang, another famous philosopher and military strategist, who used six coins to predict military events and to forecast events hundreds of years in the future. This six coin divination was called "Predictions on the Horse" because of the prominence of the horse in combat. The ten coin method of prediction originated with Chu Yan Chang, the first emperor of the Ming Dynasty. When he was a monk, during the later Yuan Dynasty (1348–1355), he used ten coins to help decide whether to escape or to join the bandits who were approaching him. He forsook both alternatives and became the leader of the revolution which toppled the Yuan Dynasty.

The use of only three coins, however, was more scholarly, more refined, and more popular. In the Ch'ing Dynasty (1644–1911), Wang Hung Shu wrote a detailed book called the *Pu Shi Ch'ing Tsung* (literally, "Orthodoxy of Prediction") to interpret results obtained with three coins. This book is still widely used by Chinese fortunetellers. It is extremely difficult, however, for Westerners to understand. The same hexagrams that appear in the *I Ching* can be found here, but only the names and without any text. The Five Elements—wood, fire, earth, metal, water—and their productive and destructive interrelationships are explained; the titles and relationships of father and son, brother and sister, husband and wife are used, as are the five symbolic animals: blue dragon, red bird, white tiger, black turtle, yellow snake.

Each generation improves on the achievements of the last. This is true even in the realm of prophecy. Coins are a development of the symbolic system. The numerical system has also advanced beyond yarrow stalks. Numerology arose, and recently I have used a new instrument, the computer, to calculate a person's destiny based on numbers which affect his life.

How to Use the Coins

Today there are people who believe the use of coins to be less formal or spiritual than the use of yarrow stalks. This is not the case; there is a spirituality connected with both the coins themselves and the method of their use.

The spiritual associations of the ancient Chinese coins used for prediction are derived from the *I Ching* itself. The Chinese coins are round with a square hole in the center; the round outer shape stands for *Ch'ien*, heaven, while the square hole represents *K'un*, earth. One side has four characters; this is the yang, or positive side. The other side originally had no characters; in the Man Ch'ing Dynasty, however, two were added—the Man Chou characters. This is the even-numbered side, representing yin, the negative. Altogether, the four added to the two stand for the six lines of the hexagrams; the total of three coins stands for heaven, earth, and man, as well as for the three lines of the trigrams. It is true that other coins are often used; I have seen coins made in Switzerland especially for prediction, with numbers and yin and yang symbols. It is quite permissible to use ordinary American coins; the "heads" side is yang, the "tails" side is yin.

No matter what coins are to be used, the same procedure should be followed. The person consulting the *I Ching* for prediction should first burn incense. One may consult either alone or with someone else who is the predictor, but in either case the person who wants an answer from the *I Ching* should pray, including his name, where he lives, what he wants, and for what purpose. He should address the *I Ching* directly, as though it were a person, asking it for instructions. Then he shakes the three coins in the smoke of the incense—these should be held in clasped palms or in a special container—and throws them on a table or some other flat surface. This ritual is no mere superstition; it has a specific purpose: to concentrate our thoughts and quiet the mind. Only when a person has clearly and definitely in his mind what he wants to know can the *I Ching* give a clear and definite answer. It is much like correctly filling out an important application form.

The hexagram is constructed from bottom to top: one line is determined by each throw of the coins. Thus, to obtain the relevant hexagram, the coins are thrown six times, with the first throw determining the bottom line and the sixth throw the top line. Starting at the bottom rather than the top is quite natural: organic things such as plants and trees are nourished through their roots. Inorganic things, too, follow this principle. Lao-tze wrote, "A tall tower nine stories high is built upon basketfuls of earth."

For each toss of the coins there are four possible combinations: (*a*) one yang (heads) and two yin (tails) sides, which equal Young Yang, an unchanging unbroken line; (*b*) one yin (tails) and two yang (heads) sides, which equal Young Yin, an unchanging broken line; (*c*) three yang (heads) sides, which equal Old Yang, a changing unbroken line; and (*d*) three yin (tails) sides, which equal Old Yin, a changing broken line. (In ancient times, the results of each toss were noted by one dot for a Young Yang line, two dots for a Young Yin line, a circle for an Old Yang line, and an X for an Old Yin line. The reader can make the dots or draw the lines directly from the coin tosses, but he should use the circles and Xs to indicate changing lines.)

A changing, or moving, line is one which changes to its opposite after the initial hexagram is obtained; an Old Yin changes to an unbroken line, and an Old Yang changes to a broken line. Thus, it is possible to receive two hexagrams of the *I Ching* in response to a single question.

After you have completed tossing the coins, you may then refer to the body of this book to receive the answer to your question. If there is no changing line, refer to the Judgment and Symbol of the hexagram you have obtained, together with the commentary I have written for it. It is not necessary to refer to any of the lines of the hexagram. If there is a changing line, refer directly to it in the section headed "The Lines" under the original hexagram obtained. Then, as a second step, refer to the new hexagram obtained when the moving line changes. Study the Judgment and Symbol of the new hexagram, for they may give you additional insight as you look for an answer to your question. It may be that there is more than one changing line. In that case, refer to all of them; but since they all change simultaneously, only one new hexagram is obtained.

When you look up particular lines, you will find that they are designated as "Nine at the bottom," "Six in the second place," "Six at the top," or the like. The number is always either six or nine. The nine indicates a yang line; nine is the sum of the three yang sides of the coins. (The four Chinese characters on the yang side, representing the four seasons in one year, are considered one unit, and assigned the number three.) The six indicates a yin line; six is the total of the characters on the yin sides of the coins. What follows the number—"at the bottom," "at the top," "in the third place,"—refers to the order of the lines in the hexagram. For example, "Nine in the second place" means an unbroken line in the place second from the bottom.

You may wonder why three yin sides together and three yang sides together constitute changing lines, lines that turn into their opposites. The reason can be found in the *I Ching* itself: "When the sun stands at midday, it begins to set; when the moon is full, it begins to wane. The fullness and emptiness of heaven and earth wane and wax in the course of time." In other words, when something reaches its high point, it changes into its opposite. Three positive coins represent the highest point of yang, which then becomes yin; the same is true for the reverse.

You may also wonder why two yang sides and one yin make a yin, or broken, line. Again this practice is derived directly from the *I Ching*; in the *Ta Chuan* it is written: "The light trigrams have more dark lines, the dark trigrams have more light lines." *Chen, K'an,* and *Ken* are the three positive trigrams, which also represent the three sons but they all consist of two Yin lines and one Yang line; the three daughters, *Sun, Li,* and *Tui,* the three negative trigrams, each has two yang and one yin line.

Sample Questions

My experience has been that the most frequent kinds of questions people ask the *I Ching* have to do with business, travel, marriage, school, or sickness. Here are some typical questions:

If I go to Europe as I plan, will good fortune or misfortune result?

I want to start a new business because the situation in my city seems good to me now. Will I succeed or not?

In starting a new enterprise, should I go to the South or to the Midwest?

When will I find love?

Will my present boyfriend/girlfriend be a good marriage partner or not?

Will I complete my studies and get my degree this summer?

Will my health improve soon?

Once a girl interested in prediction was introduced to me by one of my students in *I Ching* class. She was planning to take a trip to India, both for a vacation and to buy goods for the gift shop she owned, but she was not sure whether or not it was advisable for her to go. I had her throw the coins, and as she did she asked the *I Ching*, "Will good fortune or misfortune result from my trip?" After six tosses she obtained Hexagram 62, Slight Excess, with the moving line at the bottom (Fig. 2). The text accompanying the first line says, "A

The six coin tosses: First toss is bottom line; last toss is top line	First Hexagram: 62, Slight Excess, moving line at bottom	Second Hexagram: 55, Greatness
② ① ①	— —	— —
② ① ①	— —	— —
② ① ②	———	———
② ② ①	———	———
② ① ①	— —	— —
② ② ②	— —✕	———

1: yang side of coin / positive / heads
2: yin side of coin / negative / tails

Fig. 2

bird encounters misfortune when it soars." She asked how this related to her question, and I told her that it indicated she should not take an airplane—she should go by ship instead. When she then told me she wanted to cancel the trip completely, I advised against that, pointing out to her the new hexagram that results when the moving line changes. This is Number 55, *Feng*, Greatness, which indicates abundance in business matters—a good time to make money.

The girl had already bought her airplane ticket, but she changed her plans and went by ship. Two things happened. First, the airplane she would have flown on was hijacked to Cuba; even though there was no serious damage, the passengers were detained there for several days. And second, as a result of her purchases in India, the girl made a handsome profit.

Interpreting the Results

In this book the reader is provided with my own translations from the *I Ching* of the Judgment and Symbol of each hexagram and the text of each line. I have added my interpretations of each hexagram making use of the attributes of the trigrams and the Five Elements. Included in these interpretations are examples drawn both from my own experience with prediction and from Confucius's work *Ch'un Ch'iu*. These interpretations and examples will help the reader apply the hexagrams to his own situation. In addition, accompanying each line are specific indications of what to expect in the future; these are derived from my long contact with the wisdom of Chinese prediction.

The reader will discover that certain words recur many times, both in the translations of the texts and in my commentaries. These words have come down to us from ancient times and the reader should be acquainted with their meanings. "The superior man" who is referred to so often in the texts indicated in ancient China a person of wisdom, good nature, and high standing. In our own age one might think of a professional person of good standing, virtue, and wisdom as "the superior man."

The other words refer to the outcome of events. "Good fortune" indicates gain or success, while "misfortune" indicates loss or failure; what is gained or lost may be money, time, friends, a marriage, a job —anything important to an individual. "Humiliation" refers to strong embarrassment or shame which one suffers as a result of the situation. "No blame" means that even if a person experiences loss or suffers humiliation, he does not bear the guilt—the situation is beyond his control. "Remorse" is the result of an individual's action for which he later feels guilt and wishes he did not do. "Danger" signifies a time to be cautious of theft, accident, or other possible disasters.

In my commentaries, especially those which accompany the lines, I have tried to bring the traditional Chinese categories of prediction up to date. "Employees" were those clerks who worked for the government as civil servants; "students" or "scholars" were those people, not necessarily in school, who were studying for the official civil service examinations, or were simply waiting to get a job somewhere else. "Priests" and "monks" referred to Buddhist monks and Taoist priests, those who had special professions within religion. "Businessmen" were shopkeepers and merchants, and "farmers," of course, were those who worked the land. "Individuals" included all other people.

In this book the categories have been extended in accordance with the times. The reader consulting the lines will find indications concerning the future situation in his job or at his school as well as in his private life. The category "priests" and "monks" should be considered to include all those who work in religious organizations or institutions. Sometimes there are specific predictions for women, but otherwise the commentaries apply to women the same as to men.

The predictions accompanying the lines sometimes mention the birth time and zodiac symbols of the person bringing the question. These references are based on Chinese astrology, but Western astrology may be used if the reader is not familiar with, or does not have access to, the Chinese system.

In China, *I Ching* prediction can be very detailed. In Confucius's work *Ch'un Ch'iu,* he describes a father who asked an oracle to predict his son's future at birth. What he got was the future of the next eight generations—from one hexagram!

1. *Ch'ien / The Creative*

The first hexagram stands for heaven, the king, the leader, the father. The upper and lower primary trigrams and the two nuclear trigrams are all *Ch'ien*, indicating heaven, movement, and strength. This structure imparts to the hexagram great energy, resulting in movement: the unceasing movement of the heavens, both day and night. Through its energy heaven creates all beings, which live and die, blossom and decay. Thus the universe continues perpetually. The superior man contemplates this idea of heaven, the Creative, imitates it, and constantly tries to perfect his mental and physical powers. In so doing he contributes to society.

The Creative is the root of all the other hexagrams, because it is composed of six unbroken lines. *Ch'ien* indicates a leader or a wise and experienced man who has vitality with which to create and construct. Applying too much strength, however, produces arrogance and failure. The Creative is the strongest of the hexagrams, and if it comes to those who seek direction, they should observe caution in using their strength. Keep in mind the principles of rest and yielding.

THE JUDGMENT
The Creative brings great success,
Benefiting all through perseverance.

THE SYMBOL
Heaven moves powerfully;
The superior man strengthens himself unceasingly.

THE LINES
Nine at the bottom: The hibernating dragon does not act.

It is not a good time to be active or to commit oneself; it is, rather, a time to rest and prepare. A person can expect to retire or receive a minor position. For the businessman, activity will be slow. Only for priests, monks, and women is this line favorable: for the former there will be peace of mind, while the latter will enjoy good family relations.

Nine in the second place: The dragon is seen on the field. There is benefit in meeting a great man.

The second line denotes a time of development. People in general will be aided by those above them; those who are working will receive important jobs and get along well with intelligent superiors. During this time students and scholars will pass their exams with high grades and gain recognition, farmers' lands and fortunes will increase, merchants will prosper, and people working in religious organizations will gain high positions. A woman can expect to marry a prosperous man or get rich independently.

Nine in the third place: The superior man works creatively the whole day, and is cautious in the evening. Danger. No blame.

This is a period of disadvantage, a time of work and thinking. There is much movement without rest. One should try, however, to be cautious and not hurry. Working people can expect to be very busy with two jobs, but the unemployed will find it hard to get work. Women will experience difficulties in their relationships with men.

Nine in the fourth place: The dragon leaps from the abyss. No blame.

On the whole one can expect to encounter hard times. His doubts will cause hesitation. If a person loses his job he should wait for another; students and the unemployed should also wait for an opportunity. Women and religious persons, however, can anticipate a calm and comfortable period, and may come into some money.

Nine in the fifth place: The dragon flies in the heavens. There is benefit in meeting a great man.

One will be helped by an important or influential person to achieve his or her goal. For the unemployed this means both work and opportunity; those already employed will not be promoted, but their incomes will increase. A woman will gain the power and importance of a man in her work, but this will result in her being isolated.

If misfortune should occur, expect to go to court.

Nine at the top: The dragon is arrogant and will have cause to repent.

Arrogance leads to trouble and thus to repentance. This means that those in power are in danger of losing their friends and followers, and even with good recommendations, a person who has lost his job will have no success finding a new one. Misfortune for old men is indicated by this line. Women will either get married or have troubles with male relationships.

2. K'un / The Receptive

K'un means earth, mother, things characterized by receptivity. The upper and lower primary and nuclear trigrams are all *K'un*: earth, mother, yielding, the yin principle. The hexagram does not, however, indicate weakness. Lao-tze recognized in it the principle for his philosophy of life, that yielding can overcome strength. If you can learn to adjust to society, many people will help you. Although *K'un* is opposite in structure to *Ch'ien*, the first hexagram, it is not opposed to it. *K'un* is yin, *Ch'ien* is yang, and they cannot be separated: they are indispensable to each other and symbolize one unit. Electric current will not flow if there are only positive or negative charges.

In ancient China, *Ch'ien* stood for the king and *K'un* for the queen. In the traditional Chinese family, *K'un* represented the ideal mother. She accepted all the responsibilities of the family, performing important jobs in the home, giving birth, and raising children. She would always dispense love and kindness, in spite of hard work or unpleasantness. She was like the earth, which grows everything and receives everything back, even that which we consider dirty and ugly. It supports the mountains and cradles the oceans and never feels that it can no longer endure; neither does it complain, nor display its glory.

THE JUDGMENT

The Receptive: great success.
Benefiting from the quality of a mare—perseverance.
The superior man has an undertaking;
In the beginning he will go astray,
But later will receive guidance.
He can find a friend in the southwest
And lose friends in the northeast.
Peacefulness and continuance. Good fortune.

THE SYMBOL

The earth's condition is that of the Receptive.
The superior man has the greatness of character
To bear with everything in the world.

THE LINES

Six at the bottom: When hoarfrost is underfoot, solid ice will soon come.

Misfortune can be expected if one does not change his demeanor. Be wary of a vindictive attack: people with jobs should guard against gossip and slander, and students should guard against jealousy. During this time, however, a woman will be able to make her family prosperous.

Six in the second place: Straight, square, great—without study. Everything benefits.

This line indicates a time of benefit. Employed people will receive high promotions, the academic will gain recognition and become prosperous, wives will live harmoniously and their families will prosper. One may profitably acquire property.

Six in the third place: Hide your ability and you can continue in your position. If in public office, do not show yourself, but complete the work.

A time of quiet achievement. Working people do a good job and become eligible for promotion, the scholar writes well and soon achieves success, businessmen plan wisely and their enterprises prosper. The character and ability of a woman will grow.

Six in the fourth place: The sack is tied up. No recognition, no blame.

Keep quiet and inactive and you will not get into trouble. If your plans are interrupted, you can avoid disaster by acting cautiously.

People with jobs should be watchful, for promotions will be difficult to get, while the student will not easily find work. But women will do well in their careers and family lives owing to their good character and abilities.

Six in the fifth place: A yellow lower garment means sublime good fortune.

Everything runs smoothly and without trouble. One will receive money or other benefits—perhaps a position at headquarters. For students and scholars, it is a time of great success. For women, this is a time to develop good character and gain higher status: they will benefit their families and help their husbands' careers.

Six at the top: Dragons fight in the wilderness. The blood is black and yellow.

Expect danger. A person may be demoted or even lose his job. Even if he passes his exam, the student will not win favor. During this time beware of quarrels and lawsuits.

3. *Chun / Difficulty in the Beginning*

The third hexagram signifies difficulty or confusion in the beginning but the restoration of order later on. The upper primary trigram, *K'an*, means water, danger or difficulty, clouds, and rain; the lower primary trigram, *Chen*, means eldest son, thunder, movement. Together they present the image of clouds and thunder in the heavens: a condition of disorder. But after the rain stops, the clouds disperse, thunder ceases, and the sky becomes clear; the day is fair.

With regard to the seasons, *K'an* means winter, *Chen* spring. *K'an* can also mean water, and, of course, ice and snow; *Chen* can mean wood or grass. Thus we have the image of sprouts coming up through the frozen ground, a very hard time: difficulty in the beginning. To those who seek guidance, this hexagram means that the present time is not favorable for action. They should be patient and await the right time. A good opportunity for undertaking will eventually present itself. Difficulty in the beginning indicates later improvement: if a southeast wind or sunshine comes, the time is favorable for new sprouts, but even if the spring is harsh, the weather will eventually become warmer. You should not simply wait, however. You must also prepare.

THE JUDGMENT
Difficulty in the Beginning: great success.
It is of benefit to continue
Without planning to go someplace.
One should find helpers.

THE SYMBOL
Clouds and thunder symbolize Difficulty in the Beginning.
The superior man makes order out of disorder.

THE LINES

Nine at the bottom: Considering and considering. It is of benefit to continue in the right way. One should find helpers.

Act only with caution, but remember that hesitation now can lead to trouble later; one can remain stable without haste or failure.

Working people will do their jobs well and receive important positions. People in school will receive help from a superior and succeed. For women, good character, successful careers, and families are indicated.

Six in the second place: Many difficulties. He goes back and forth on horseback, but he is not a robber. He seeks marriage but the girl does not want an engagement. After ten years she does.

Now is a good time for people to change their careers to highly competitive ones—perhaps in the military—and thus become powerful. It is also the time for a person to get married or gain a friend. Students and scholars, however, will not easily find jobs. If birth time and zodiac symbols are not favorable, one will meet obstacles —perhaps a lawsuit—and it will be hard to achieve one's goal.

Six in the third place: He hunts deer with a forester. He gets lost in the forest. The superior man, knowing this, prefers to give up the hunt. To go on would bring regret.

To act now may lead to dishonor, dismissal, or demotion; rather it is a time to be quiet and refrain from action. One should also be wary of being detained by someone in trouble. A student may expect difficulty which will hinder his progress.

Six in the fourth place: He goes back and forth on horseback. If he seeks marriage, he will have good fortune. Everything benefits.

This line indicates good fortune and advantage in every way: one will live harmoniously and achieve one's goals. Working people can expect high salaries, recognition, and the chance for promotion, while the student will easily get a job to his liking. Women who want to marry will find good husbands and have fine children.

Nine in the fifth place: Difficulties in prosperity. Good fortune for small things. Misfortune for great things.

Now is the time to plan carefully. Misconduct leads to trouble, but caution can avoid it.

Six at the top: He goes back and forth on horseback. He sheds tears with blood!

Arrogance leads to misfortune, perhaps extreme misfortune. At work you should guard against jealousy and slander, no matter how high your position or connections; at school you should be wary of receiving insult.

Keep a check on the health of your parents.

4. *Meng / Youth*

Youthful folly, an immature condition, is signified by the fourth hexagram. *Meng* also refers to the education of the young. The upper trigram is *Ken*, the lower trigam *K'an*. Here *K'an* means water or danger; *Ken* means mountain or the youngest: the stream of water, *K'an*, is just coming out from the foot of the mountain, *Ken*. This image indicates a purity like the minds of children, which are blank. One can direct them to do both good and evil; thus the task of educating youth is a holy one. Accordingly, one should teach children to act in the correct way. The Judgment says, "The first time he asks, I answer; but if he asks again and again . . . no answer."

Applied to using the *I Ching*, this means that there is only one hexagram for one question—you should ask your question only once, or you will not receive the correct answer.

To those who seek direction, this hexagram indicates that they should be more thoughtful. If someone misunderstands you, you should explain clearly and patiently what you mean. Treat people generously. In this way will you meet with great success.

THE JUDGMENT

It is not I who seek him,
The youth seeks me.
The first time he asks, I answer;
But if he asks again and again,
It is annoyance: no answer.
Benefit for continuance.

THE SYMBOL

A spring comes out at the foot of the mountain;
This symbolizes Youth.
The superior man will cultivate his character
Through decisive action.

THE LINES

Six at the bottom: To enlighten youth, it is better to use discipline. Obstacles in the mind should be removed. Otherwise, humiliation.

One will encounter gossip, disputes, perhaps even lawsuits, and will be liable to fall out of harmony with one's friends or family, but in the end will be free of entanglements. The student can expect to pass his exams and start a new career.

This is a good time for people to find opportunities in education or law.

Nine in the second place: To treat youth generously brings good fortune. Arranging a marriage brings good fortune. The son can take over the household.

Conditions will be peaceful, and one may be either active or at rest. A person will keep his job, be in harmony with society, and easily achieve his undertakings; in addition he can expect to associate with a great or important personality. Perhaps marriage and children are indicated. Students should look to teaching careers for fulfillment.

Six in the third place: Do not choose a girl who, when she sees a rich man, loses her control. No benefit.

Now it is best to be quiet and cautious, otherwise one will be caught up in gossip. A man should beware of failure due to trouble with women or with drinking. People should avoid bribery at work, and students should guard against wasting study time.

Six in the fourth place: The youth beset by confusion. Humiliation.

Be quiet and cautious; do not get lost by taking action thoughtlessly. You may have trouble getting along with other people at this time, and your enterprises may not go smoothly. If employed, your chances are not good for promotion; if a student, lack of recommendations will make it hard to get a job.

Six in the fifth place: The youth submits. Good fortune.

If you receive this line, you can expect to achieve your goals easily.

Nine at the top: To punish youth, it does no good to commit a violation. The idea is to prevent a violation.

Caution is advised. At this time there may be disputes, lawsuits, thefts, or slander from those below. Students, however, can expect to achieve their goals and gain rewards, and working people may obtain jobs related to the government.

5. *Hsu / Waiting (Nourishment)*

Hsu means necessity, nourishment, or waiting. The upper trigram is *K'an*—water or danger; the lower is *Ch'ien*—heaven, sky, or strength. The image is that of water in the heavens: it is cloudy and it will rain, but you cannot make it rain; you must wait. Thus the hexagram indicates waiting, but not idly: one should use this time to prepare for the future.

Nourishment here also means good opportunity. Those who get this hexagram should be ambitious; there will be good fortune in seeking transfer and advancement. Proceed step by step, not rapidly; be careful, but not afraid. Competition at this time can be a beneficial thing. According to the fifth line, you will be successful through effort with caution. The sixth line indicates that you should treat friends, colleagues, even enemies, generously.

This hexagram also refers to meditation. The Chinese character for *Hsu* pictures a man sitting with his spine erect, his hands and legs crossed, on a four-legged bench. Nourishment in this case is the reserve of inner energy in the meditator's abdomen. The Decision says, "If you are sincere, you will have glory (light) and success. . . . It is of benefit to cross the great water (to travel to remote places)." If you persevere with meditation and await the rising of energy, you will see your glory. Crossing the great water means the passing of the essence from the pelvic flower up the spinal cord to the top of the head.

THE JUDGMENT

Waiting. If you are sincere
You will have glory (light) and success.
Continuing leads to good fortune.

It is of benefit to cross the great water (to travel to remote places).

THE SYMBOL
Clouds rise up in the sky;
This symbolizes Waiting.
The superior man enjoys his food and drink.
He remains relaxed and happy.

THE LINES
Nine at the bottom: Waiting in the countryside. It is of benefit to continue. No regret.

Even if one has some success, he will not be satisfied with his situation. But now is the time to avoid adventuresome undertakings and to work instead at maintaining one's position.

Nine in the second place: Waiting in the sand (seashore, bank of the river) arouses gossip. Good fortune in the end.

A time of agitation: one will be involved in disputes or lawsuits and disturbed by gossip. Both teachers and students are liable to become the objects of blame because of either their work or their exams. But if one treats others generously, everything will resolve itself.

This is the time to consider a job involving speaking.

Nine in the third place: Waiting in the mud brings on the enemy.

Everyone should be wary of theft or loss of possessions. If a person should lose his job, it will be his own fault. A student should guard against slander.

Caution in traveling is advised.

Six in the fourth place: Waiting in blood. Come out from the pit.

The situation is troublesome, but it will gradually become peaceful; freedom follows entrapment. A person can now better his position at work while avoiding danger, and students can get their degrees, but great success remains beyond reach.

Nine in the fifth place: Waiting at the feast. Continuing brings good fortune.

At this time you can expect to gain property or money, or you may get married. If you work you will get a job at headquarters or become the head of a branch.

This is also a time of eating good food.

Six at the top: Entering the pit, three unexpected guests arrive. Treat them courteously. Good fortune in the end.

Proceed slowly and be extremely cautious, otherwise you are destined for misery and sickness. When you enter headquarters, beware of slander. If you are a student, you might do advanced study, but others are likely to suspect your motives.

6. *Sung / Conflict*

A conflict, argument, or dispute is indicated by *Sung*. The upper primary trigram is *Ch'ien*, which signifies both strength and movement; the lower primary trigram is *K'an*, water, which indicates danger. Heaven implies an upward movement, but the natural movement of water is downward: the opposite nature of these forces is the basis for conflict.

Ch'ien also stands for an old man or leader; *K'an* stands for a young man. This means that when there is conflict, the young man should consult the older man who has more experience than he does. The older man is like a wise leader who can instruct his followers.

Those who get this hexagram should not attempt any great undertakings in business or anything else. If one maintains the present conditions, he can expect good fortune. Prospects for an intended marriage or love affair are not favorable.

THE JUDGMENT
Conflict; you have sincerity
Even though obstructed,
Stop halfway—good fortune;
Follow to the end—misfortune.
It is of benefit to see the great man,
But not to cross the great water.

THE SYMBOL
Heaven and water go in different directions,
Symbolizing Conflict.
The superior man contemplates the beginning
Before undertaking an enterprise.

THE LINES
Six at the bottom: One does not continue the affair (conflict). Even if there is some gossip, good fortune in the end.

Although the first line indicates a time of gossip, lawsuits, and disaster, it also suggests that all will end well. People will meet with slander in their jobs, but it will disappear without their answering; students are talked about, but that comes to nothing. The sick will recover without medication. If birth time and zodiac symbols are unfavorable, however, one will suffer from poor health.

Nine in the second place: One cannot continue the conflict. Retreating, he goes home. Three hundred families in his town will avoid disaster.

People who remain with their families will live in peace without danger. Those employed can expect higher salaries; those in school will have stability. But if misfortune should occur, one will have to go to a faraway place or take part in a lawsuit or divorce proceeding.

Six in the third place: Depending upon ancient virtues. Continuing in this way leads to danger. In the end, good fortune. While working in public affairs, one should not seek achievement.

During this time people can expect to maintain their normal daily lives. This means no advancement, but no failure or difficulty either.

Nine in the fourth place: One cannot continue the conflict. Returning and changing one's attitude brings peace and good fortune.

Now is a time of peace, good fortune, and comfort, a good time to improve your conduct. If you lose your job you will find another; if now in school, you will find an opportunity to obtain a new position. But if birth time and zodiac symbols are unfavorable, you should beware of others bothering you.

Nine in the fifth place: Conflict. To submit the conflict to a great man brings great good fortune.

One can expect to make money from his undertaking. The employed person can look forward to an important position, and the student will pass an exam and gain recognition.

Nine at the top: Even if he receives an ornamental belt, it will be snatched away three times in one morning.

A time of conflict or mourning. For working people this line indicates some success, some failure: they may advance, then decline. But students will pass their exams with very high grades.

7. *Shih / The Army*

Shih signifies an army, a battle, competition, or business rivalry. The upper primary trigram is *K'un*, representing earth, soil, or masses of people; the lower primary trigram is *K'an*, representing water or danger. When water collects in the earth, it becomes a powerful force, as people assembled in an army are powerful. But if there is too much water, it will erode the earth and overflow, causing damage. So, too, must the army be carefully trained, or disorder and rebellion will erupt. It should be loyal and work for the benefit of the country.

The unbroken line in the second place indicates the general. All the other lines are broken, or yielding: they give to the general the power necessary to do his job. The success of an army in battle depends on both the degree of trust the soldiers place in their general, and the general's confidence in the ability and loyalty of his troops. By his conduct and morals, he should strive to win the respect of the army and the people; he should demonstrate his wisdom through generosity. The same is true for business. The manager must strive to win the confidence of employee and owner alike.

THE JUDGMENT
The Army. The army demands perseverance
And a strong person (leader).
Good fortune. No blame.

THE SYMBOL
Water in the earth
Symbolizes the Army.
The superior man increases his followers
By benevolence toward the people.

THE LINES

Six at the bottom: An army should be put in correct order. If not, there will be disaster.

The time is favorable for one to make money through smart undertakings. Those employed will see their work go smoothly and will gain the favor of their superiors; students and scholars will pursue the correct course of study and achieve their goals. But if a person is rude and thoughtless, he will fail more often than not. Watch out for danger or disease.

Nine in the second place: A general works within his army. Good fortune, no blame. The king confers a triple honor.

People can expect to be helped by influential persons to achieve their goals. Those employed will be honored and receive important positions, or they will change their careers. Students will earn high grades on their examinations. Women, priests, and monks will all be honored.

Six in the third place: The army carries corpses. Misfortune.

This is a time of sudden mourning. People born in the twelfth month (January), however, will have good fortune.

If you are looking for a job, you can expect to be put on a waiting list, but the job will provide little money or benefits.

Six in the fourth place: The army retreats at the proper time. No blame.

By avoiding reckless action, a person will have a comfortable life and enjoy his career. This is a good time to repair one's home or to travel.

It may be better to decline a job offer now. But a student can expect an award.

Six in the fifth place: Much game in the field. It benefits to capture it. No blame. The army is led by the eldest son. The younger son carries corpses. Continuing brings misfortune.

People will add to their property, achieve their goals, and find good helpers. Those employed can look forward to more power and a better position, and students can expect to pass their exams and be successful.

One should be wary, however, for trouble to one's youngest son.

Six at the top: The king issues directives, establishes states, and awards fiefs to certain families. Inferiors should not be given power.

At this time people can expect to attain prosperity for their families. Those employed will gain the power to achieve their career goals, while those who are self-employed will gain recognition through their skills. But one should beware of gossip and one's own arrogance, for these can bring misfortune.

8. *Pi / Union*

Pi means harmony, cooperation, or merging of separate parts. The upper trigram is *K'an*, water, and the lower is *K'un*, earth: water on the earth. The earth receives the water and the water moistens the earth. There is a close bond between them, like the relationship between mother and child.

The preceding hexagram, *Shih*, represented a time of war when the leader was in the second position, far from the ruler; in *Pi* the leader is in the fifth place, a high position. All the other lines are broken and subordinate to the unbroken one; the person indicated possesses generosity and a strong character.

This hexagram is good fortune for those who can cooperate and act with sincerity. It is favorable for love and marriage. For business, it means prosperity and good fortune, if the manager is honest and forthright. Where there is mutual trust, undertakings will be successful, but trust develops only when people act guilelessly.

THE JUDGMENT
Union: good fortune.
The prediction for one attempting union
Should be greatness, continuation, and constancy;
No blame.
If one hesitates, then joins late: misfortune.

THE SYMBOL
Water over the earth
Symbolizes Union.
The ancient kings established many states
And were friendly with feudal lords.

THE LINES
Six at the bottom: Union with confidence. No blame.
Full of confidence, like a bowl full of water. Good
fortune in the end.

People will get help from friends to achieve their goals easily. Those who are working will receive an unexpected promotion; the student will find a job through a recommendation.

Six in the second place: Union from within. Continuing
brings good fortune.

With help from important persons, people will achieve their goals. Students and scholars can expect recognition and a position, and women are likely to find good husbands. At work, however, one may be on a trial period.

Six in the third place: Union with the wrong people.
There will be sad results.

This is a time of conflict, mourning, lost money, or exile to a remote place. A woman is in danger of marrying an unworthy husband, thus damaging herself and her family. A student may be suspended or expelled. Everyone should watch out for jealous or suspicious friends and beware of declining health.

Six in the fourth place: Union outside. Continuing brings good fortune.

People succeed with the help of friends and easily achieve their goals. Those with jobs can expect to be promoted.

Nine in the fifth place: Union with honor. The king hunts on three sides only, losing game through the front. The people are not afraid. Good fortune.

Obstruction in the beginning, smoothness later: people can expect success in their enterprises and comfort in their personal lives. The employee can look forward to promotion, and the student can expect to receive a fellowship or an academic degree.

Six at the top: Union without a leader. Misfortune.

This is a time of trouble and difficulties: people cannot get along with their friends, and they may suffer from poor health as well. At work one is liable to meet a dangerous situation with no support from his friends. Without help from the school administration, the student will find it difficult to gain recognition.

9. *Hsiao Ch'u / Taming the Small Powers*

Taming the Small Powers implies rest, storage, and preparation. The upper trigram is *Sun*, wind, the lower is *Ch'ien*, heaven or sky, while the nuclear trigrams are *Li*, the sun, and *Tui*, clouds: the wind blows and clouds accumulate in the sky, covering up the sun. It is going to rain, but not yet. This situation symbolizes the preparation which precedes a new development; after battle—Hexagram 7—comes unification—Hexagram 8—and then rest and preparation.

Hsiao Ch'u is favorable for new undertakings. Although there may be confusion and difficulty, one should be patient, for success will come in the end. For love and marriage, this hexagram indicates temporary trouble and suspicion which will eventually be resolved.

THE JUDGMENT
Taming the Small Powers: Success.
Thick clouds come from the west. No rain.

THE SYMBOL
The wind blows across the sky,
Symbolizing Taming the Small Powers.
The superior man improves his ability and virtue.

THE LINES
Nine at the bottom: Return to the correct way. Then how can one be blamed? It is good fortune.

This line signifies a time of peace. The person without a job will find one, the wanderer will return to his home, and the student will go back to his studies. But if birth time and zodiac symbols are unfavorable, one will hesitate and find it difficult to make decisions. A person should avoid suspicion and jealousy in any new undertaking.

Nine in the second place: One is influenced to return to the correct way. Good fortune.

Now is the time for people to unite and achieve their goals. Those employed can expect to become supervisors and be recommended for new positions, and those in the academic world will give distinguished performances and advance before their peers. But if birth time and zodiac symbols are not favorable, one may become entangled in one's mistakes and fail.

Nine in the third place: The wheels separate from the wagon. Husband and wife are in disharmony.

Even if conditions seem favorable, you are now in danger of being slandered. Do not expect a promotion, but rather, prepare for setbacks. At this time a person should watch out for disease in the feet or eyes. There may be a separation from one's family.

Six in the fourth place: If you are forthright, bloodshed and fear vanish; no blame.

This line indicates that a person will be in harmony with his circle of friends because of his honesty and that he will succeed in his enterprises. For the working person this means a promotion with the recommendation of his friends and colleagues. The student will have the favor of those above him and the means to achieve his goal. But if birth time and zodiac symbols are unfavorable, there is danger of bloodshed.

Nine in the fifth place: If you are sincere you will be enriched by your neighbor.

You can expect help from others and you will slowly achieve success. Relied on by his employer and appreciated by his friends, the employee will find his position increasing in importance. Scholars will achieve cooperation in working toward a common goal.

Nine at the top: It is raining; one can rest, respected for one's virtues. Continuing to hesitate like a woman brings danger; the moon is almost full. If the superior man sets forth, misfortune.

If you withdraw you can avoid the troubles indicated by this line. Rivals will try to trap you or get you fired; watch out for gossip. If you are a student you are in danger of being slandered because of your beliefs.

10. *Lu / Treading*

The tenth hexagram gives advice on how one should act. *Tui*, the youngest daughter, follows in the footsteps of *Ch'ien*, the father, the upper trigram; thus she avoids mistakes. But *Tui* also means tiger, and we have here another image: someone stepping on the tiger's tail. Gentleness in this situation is indicated, however, by *Sun*, the upper nuclear trigram, which is the gentle. In addition, the lower nuclear trigram is *Li*, which can denote the eyes: one looks very carefully when stepping on the tiger's tail. In a dangerous situation you should act very cautiously, thus escaping harm. If you decide to follow the ideas or advice of a wise man, you should first contemplate the meaning of those ideas in the context of your own life.

To those who seek prediction, this hexagram advises quietness and inactivity. You should act only after you have planned carefully, and then with resolution. In seclusion you will receive good fortune or at least avoid disaster. The second, fourth, and sixth lines are favorable because they are in yielding positions, the third is bad fortune, the fifth line, even though in a central position, is still dangerous.

On December 12, 1936, Generalissimo Chiang Kai-shek was taken prisoner by his own rebelling generals in Shi-an, China. The country was shocked. People consulted the *I Ching* to find out what would happen, and this hexagram appeared, with the moving line in the fourth position. I advised that there was no need to worry, that General Chiang would be released. (The fourth line says, "He steps on the tail of the tiger. Caution and fearfulness. Good fortune in the end.") Two weeks later, on Christmas day, General Chiang was set free and he returned to Nanking. Curiously enough, the name of one of the rebelling generals was Yang Hu Ch'eng; *Hu* means "tiger," *Ch'eng* means "city"; literally, the name means "tiger city."

THE JUDGMENT
Treading: Stepping on the tail of a tiger,
But it does not bite one. Success.

THE SYMBOL
The heaven above and the lake below
Symbolize Treading.
The superior man differentiates between high and low,
And thus fixes the minds of the people.

THE LINES
Nine at the bottom: Simplicity of conduct. Continue. No blame.

People can expect to achieve their goals and in the process make money. If the employed person is conscientious and generous, he will have a good chance for promotion. If the student receives good training, he will be successful.

Nine in the second place: Treading in a safe and peaceful way. The man in seclusion carries on. Good fortune.

Caution will bring good fortune. Although students and scholars have little chance for gaining a new position, they should be content. This is a good time for a working person to retire.

Six in the third place: A one-eyed man can see; a lame man can walk. But when they step on the tail of a tiger, the tiger will bite. Misfortune. The warrior conducts himself like a great prince.

This is a dangerous time: watch out for conflicts, lawsuits, imprisonment, bankruptcy. If you work, you are in danger of losing your job; if you are in school, you should be wary of slanderous attacks.

Nine in the fourth place: He steps on the tail of the tiger. Caution and fearfulness. Good fortune in the end.

Trouble or disaster threaten and one must be very careful. Women will not get along with their husbands and families; working people will have little influence. The student, however, will pass his exams with high grades.

Nine in the fifth place: Continue in a decisive manner. Danger.

There is now a tendency to rush and be careless. By all means stop this, or troubles will mount and disaster will come. Working people will achieve a great deal but will gain neither recognition nor reward.

Nine at the top: Observe your conduct and examine the signs carefully. There will be great good fortune.

You can expect to receive money or property. If you have retired from a high position, you will find peace and comfort. If a student, you will improve yourself and achieve success. Do not listen to the advice of others.

11. *T'ai / Peace*

T'ai is a hexagram of good fortune; it indicates a time of peace, prosperity, flowering, and harmony. The upper trigram, *K'un*, is earth, masses, flexibility, and mother; the lower trigram, *Ch'ien,* is strength, father, king, or leader. Their position in this hexagram indicates a leader who is humble before the people, flexible and yielding on the outside but internally strong and with great energy. The upper nuclear trigram, *Chen*, stands for wood, and the lower nuclear trigram, *Tui,* for lake. Together they present the image of trees growing beside a lake: nourished by the water, the trees grow well. *Chen* also means spring, and *Tui* autumn, good times for growth and harvest.

K'un, the upper trigram, is female, or yielding; *Ch'ien,* the lower, is male, or strong. Thus the male obeys the female: the strong yields to the weak. This indicates a person whose inner purpose is very definite, but who acts externally with moderation. Those who get this hexagram have the ability to live harmoniously with their friends and colleagues on all levels of society: everything they do will go smoothly. In the family there will be harmony between husband and wife.

T'ai forecasts success. If you do something well, however, don't become intoxicated by success, for then arrogance and downfall will be the final results. This is the warning of the sixth line.

THE JUDGMENT
Peace. The small is departing,
The great is arriving.
Good fortune. Success.

THE SYMBOL
Heaven and earth are unified, symbolizing Peace.
The ruler reforms and completes
The way of heaven and earth;
He observes the appropriate methods of heaven and earth
To direct the people.

THE LINES
Nine at the bottom: When ribbon grass is pulled out, its roots come with it: they are of the same kind. Undertakings lead to good fortune.

By cooperating with friends, one will make more money, day by day. For the workingman this means harmony at work and a good chance for promotion. If students perform with honesty and ability, they will have great opportunities for success.

Nine in the second place: Bear with the undeveloped. Swim across the river decisively, not forgetting what is remote, nor disregarding one's friends. Thus one can gain the middle way.

This line indicates that one will have the support of an important person; it also means success in a remote place or a period of self-employment for someone who works. People in the academic world will be successful, gaining recognition, benefits, and money from their undertakings. But if birth time and zodiac symbols are not favorable, a person will lose the advantages he has accrued or get into trouble through a dispute.

Nine in the third place: No plain without a slope. No departure without a return. Continuing in difficult situation. No blame. Do not fear; face the truth. One receives blessings.

This is a time to be cautious and to maintain the present position of you and your family. Avoid difficult situations, otherwise you will be entrapped amid obstacles and insults. At work you should fulfill your duties carefully, thus preventing jealousy and slander. If in school, you should keep your present course. Do not expect good fortune.

Six in the fourth place: One strives with a cheerful manner, not boasting of riches to a neighbor. One has full confidence without fear.

One should not expect to achieve one's undertakings: if an enterprise is begun, it will fail. People will gossip about you. If you retire, your troubles will end.

Six in the fifth place: The Emperor I gives his daughter in marriage. This will bring blessings and great good fortune.

As the text says, this is a time of "great good fortune." Employed people will have favorable opportunities for promotion and success; students will pass important exams and get their degrees. Some can expect to become famous and win the favor of society. Perhaps others will marry and have a child.

Six at the top: The wall collapses into the moat. Do

not use force. Make announcements to the people in your own town. Continuing will bring humiliation.

This is not a good time: working people are in danger of being demoted or dismissed, students of being slandered, and people in general of suffering loss and sickness. But if one is kind and generous, he will avoid disaster.

12. *P'i / Stagnation*

This hexagram is the opposite of the preceding one, Peace; it means stagnation, poverty, or hard times. The upper trigram is *Ch'ien*—strength, leader, or king; the lower trigram is *K'un*, meaning yielding or masses. Together they indicate something strong on top but weak below which will easily collapse. Referring to persons, the trigram *Ch'ien* indicates someone strong or proud on the outside, while *K'un* means weakness within, like a person who hides his emptiness behind cleverness or arrogance. He does not get along with people anywhere, either at home or in society, and thus falls upon hard times. He is also like the leader who appears proud and powerful in public but who is actually a weak ruler whom the masses will overthrow, unlike the yielding ruler of Hexagram 11. This was the fate of Louis XVI of France, a tyrant who provoked the French Revolution.

If you get this hexagram do not be discouraged. If you change your attitude and manner, you can improve your condition. The writings of Lao-tze express this idea: good fortune is often hidden in misfortune; misfortune sometimes lies in good fortune. People who are poor but who work and study diligently can become rich and prosperous. When you decide to act, make sure you have planned well and that you act with moderation; thus the situation can be turned to the good. (See fifth and sixth lines below.)

THE JUDGMENT

Stagnation. Stagnation is of no benefit,
Although not of man's doing.
The superior man carries on (according to his principles).
The great is departing,
The small is arriving.

THE SYMBOL

Heaven and earth are not united,
Symbolizing Stagnation.
The superior man restrains himself to avoid danger.
He seeks neither honor nor wealth.

THE LINES

Six at the bottom: When ribbon grass is pulled out, its roots come with it. They are of the same kind. Continuing leads to success and good fortune.

A person who gets this line should be circumspect and avoid involvement with people of evil intention. If looking for work, one should await a vacancy; if already working, avoid gossip. The scholar will have difficulty getting a position at this time.

Six in the second place: Forbearance and obedience bring good fortune for the inferior. The superior man is stagnant. But his purpose will succeed.

If you remain humble you will be safe, for in its confusion and disorder society will condemn all prominent persons. If working, be cautious; if in school, bide your time.

Six in the third place: They bear with humiliation.

Now is the time to avoid gossip, insult, and humiliation, especially if you are a student.

An employed person is likely to resign his position.

Nine in the fourth place: He whose actions are in accord with the orders of the highest receives no blame. His fellows share in his blessing.

People can expect to receive property, and both they and their descendants will have good fortune. Those employed will receive a raise and a promotion through a friend's help, while those in school will gain recognition by someone's recommendation.

Nine in the fifth place: Stagnation is coming to an end. The great man has good fortune. "Will it fail, will it fail?" He ties it to the mulberry shoots.

Sadness becomes happiness; misfortune turns to good fortune. People will be troublefree, a jealous rival will be silenced, and a windfall will come in the form of property. Those employed will have important positions, but if birth time and zodiac symbols are not favorable they will lose them.

Nine at the top: Stagnation ends. First there is stagnation, later good fortune.

For a long time one should expect difficulty: he may lose his job or be set back in school. Later, however, the situation will improve: one will find another job or advance in school. A drawn-out legal suit will be won eventually. But if birth time and zodiac symbols are unfavorable there may be sadness and illness.

13. *T'ung Jen / Fellowship of Men*

T'ung Jen signifies union, cooperation, or a group of people working together for the same end. The sun (*Li*, the lower trigram) is shining brightly in the heavens (*Ch'ien*, the upper trigram), lighting and benefiting the whole world. *Li* also denotes fire, warmth, and clarity, and *Ch'ien* strength and decisiveness: together they indicate a person decisive on the outside, warm and clear-minded on the inside. Those who get this hexagram have a capacity for leadership: the ability to organize businesses, political parties, or other groups.

In such undertakings there will be many competitors and even danger, but in the end, success.

If you get this hexagram you should avoid conflict: yield and have patience. Both the upper primary and upper nuclear trigrams are *Ch'ien*, which indicates great strength and an excess of energy. The lower nuclear trigram, *Sun*, is wind, and lower primary trigram, *Li*, is fire. The wind blows the fire, causing it to burn higher: you easily become angry and excited because of the raging fire within. When *T'ung Jen* changes from positive to negative it becomes Hexagram 7, *Shih,* the Army, or battle.

One of my students owned shares of stock that declined sharply in 1971. She became very upset, almost hysterical. When she turned to the *I Ching* for prediction she got this hexagram, with the fifth line as the moving line. I told her not to worry, that she would not lose her money but, rather, would receive benefits. The next year her stocks rose, and she not only regained the loss but made a profit as well.

THE JUDGMENT
Fellowship of men in the open (countryside).
Success.
It benefits one to cross the great water.
It benefits the superior man to continue his task.

THE SYMBOL
Fire goes up to heaven,
Symbolizing Fellowship of Men.
The superior man organizes his kinship group (party),
And sorts them out.

THE LINES
Nine at the bottom: Fellowship of men outside the gate.
No blame.

Good friends will cooperate in undertakings for your benefit. Either a long trip or repairs in the home are in store. The employee will have a better chance for promotion; the student will get a degree and easily obtain a position.

Six in the second place: Fellowship of men in the kinship group (party). Humiliation.

One can expect unsettled affairs. Differing tastes will lead to trouble with relatives and friends, with jealousy and gossip the result. The employee will be locked into his present job and cannot expect a salary increase. The student will graduate, but he will not find success at his job.

Nine in the third place: They hide arms in the bushes. They climb to the summit of a hill. For three years they do not act.

For most people this is a time of disputes and mourning. Only with caution can one avoid losing his job. For students and scholars, however, the line indicates that a high position is forthcoming.

Nine in the fourth place: They climb on the wall. They are unable to attack. Good fortune.

A person can expect greater responsibility in his job, or he may be involved in constructing a building. He will be rewarded for his good work. A student, however, will not be able to find employment.

If you are successful at this time, you may also encounter suspicion, jealousy, insults, and conflict. Take precautions.

Nine in the fifth place: Fellowship of men. They cry and lament. Later they laugh. After great battles they have success.

Happiness and work come and go; people will have difficulty in the beginning but easy going later on—including a promotion.

At this time one has good prospects for a career involving speaking.

Nine at the top: Fellowship of men in the open (countryside). No remorse.

Nine at the top indicates that work in a remote place is likely. But if you don't have a job already, it will be difficult to find one. The correct course is to keep your old position and lead a settled life.

14. *Ta Yu / Great Possessions*

Riches, wealth, and success are all indicated by *Ta Yu,* whose upper trigram is *Li* (sun, glory, clarity) and lower trigram is *Ch'ien* (heaven and strength). The great man's honor and glory can enlighten society as the noonday sun shines on the earth. The upper and lower nuclear trigrams signify gold. *Ta Yu* indicates an initial setback to one's plans, such as jealousy or losing a small sum of money, but in the end success.

This hexagram also applies as a warning to the person who has already achieved great success. Almost all the six lines are favorable, but one must remember that misfortune often hides in good fortune. Even as the sun reaches its zenith at noon, it is beginning to set; when the moon is full it begins to wane. So too if a man is rich and pursues indulgent luxury, he will gradually become poor, and when a man is successful, he may easily become arrogant, lose his friends, and develop enemies and rivals. With a correct attitude, however, he can retain his prosperity. The next hexagram is *Ch'ien,* or Modesty—if a man is modest, then he will gain Happiness, the sixteenth hexagram, *Yu.*

THE JUDGMENT
Great Possessions.
Great Success.

THE SYMBOL
Fire over heaven symbolizes Great Possessions.
The superior man suppresses evil and honors virtue,
And thus follows the will of heaven and waits upon destiny.

THE LINES
Nine at the bottom: Avoidance of the harmful brings no blame. Awareness of difficulty—also no blame.

This line indicates sadness and confusion but also that one can avoid them by being cautious. Perhaps a person should resign his job before misfortune strikes, even though he is now satisfied. For the academic, no new accomplishments are likely now. Leaders should beware of insults from inferiors.

Nine in the second place: Loading the big wagon. Undertaking without blame.

One can expect to achieve his undertaking and acquire property. This means that working people will receive important positions, students will advance, and the military will achieve victory. For older people, however, the line means poor health.

Nine in the third place: A duke makes an offering to the emperor. The inferior man is unable to do this.

Working people can expect important positions, but the academic will find it hard to advance and may be insulted by those below him.
If birth time and zodiac symbols are unfavorable, one will not get along with his colleagues and maybe punished or injured.

Nine in the fourth place: He distinguishes between himself and his friends. This brings no blame.

Durign this time you will maintain your present position without great difficulty. Trouble may develop, however, in the eyes.

Six in the fifth place: One is confident, sociable, and dignified. Good fortune.

Proud or aggressive actions will cause trouble. One should not be hasty but wait for the proper opportunity to act. The employed person should consider resigning before unfavorable events occur. But for the academic, if the time is favorable, an enterprise should be undertaken.

Nine at the top: One is blessed by heaven. Good fortune. Benefit in everything.

This line signifies a period when everyone advances, favored by important persons in high positions. The farmer will be prosperous.

15. Ch'ien / Modesty

The image presented by *Ch'ien* is that of the mountain *(Ken)* below the earth *(K'un)*. It also represents the period between winter and spring, when nature stores its energy within while the outside is cold and barren. Thus this hexagram indicates a person who is wealthy and recognized but who is humble and polite, not only to superiors, but also to subordinates. In this attitude he gets along well with people everywhere.

Ch'ien is made up of one positive (yang) line and five negative (yin) lines. For a man this means he will get along well with women; for a woman it indicates ability to manage a household. Her husband would do well to listen to her ideas.

In the *I Ching* the positive and negative forces—the forceful and the yielding—are constantly interchanging. Applied to *Ch'ien* the interchange means that a humble person should sometimes change his manner by gathering strength and taking the offensive. Perhaps it is necessary that he defend himself against those who would take advantage of his humility.

THE JUDGMENT
Modesty: success.
The superior man can continue his work to the end.

THE SYMBOL
The mountain within the earth symbolizes Modesty.

The superior man reduces the excess and increases the
  lacking;
He weighs and then equalizes all things.

THE LINES

Six at the bottom: The superior man is modest in his
modesty. It is favorable to cross the great water. Good
fortune.

Six at the bottom suggests travel to a remote place. If you work
you can expect added responsibilities. If you are in school you will
demonstrate knowledge and ability, and you should wait for the right
career opportunity.

But if birth time and zodiac symbols are not favorable, you may
suffer injury.

Six in the second place: Modesty is expressed. Continuing
brings good fortune.

One should keep his position and not act abruptly. Working
people will have a chance for promotion; those without jobs will
achieve their undertakings.

Nine in the third place: The superior man works in a
modest way to conclusion. Good fortune.

People will profit by their undertakings and lead active lives.
Those employed will have favorable opportunities for advancement.

Six in the fourth place: To act with modesty is beneficial
toward everything.

Be humble and avoid harm. Employed people can expect good
fortune in all things. But students, farmers, merchants, and self-
employed businessmen should remain as they are and not undertake new enterprises.

Six in the fifth place: Do not show off your riches to your
neighbor. It is beneficial to attack with force. It is
favorable for everything.

This line indicates that people will gain great benefits and be
successful through the help of important persons. They should, how-

ever, beware of conflict. It also implies that a person might find himself especially suited for a position in the military or in law. Students can expect to pass their exams and receive their degrees.

Six at the top: Modesty is expressed. It is favorable to use the army to chastise the city and country.

Conflict will upset you, but resolution will follow. You can avoid remorse and failure by using your intelligence, but your mind must be tranquil. You can also expect to get a job with greater independence. A student can expect to gain recognition within his circle, even though he completes his course with few honors.

16. *Yu / Happiness*

Yu, the name of this hexagram, means both happiness and preparation, and it implies enthusiasm. The period between winter and spring is represented, when the first thunder (*Chen*, the upper trigram) awakens all creatures and plants on the earth (*K'un*). *K'un* also signifies the mother, who here is giving birth to her first son, *Chen*. Thus it is a time of new undertakings and great happiness.

Receivers of this hexagram should be wary of exhibiting excessive enthusiasm when beginning a new undertaking. If they are not, there will be misfortune. The hexagram also advises that everything necessary for advancement should be made ready. Then if an opportunity presents itself, it should be seized immediately, without hesitation. The third line indicates disappointment if this is not done. The fourth line suggests great success and wealth. But beware: indulgence can ruin health—the fifth line says that there will be persistent illness. Everything should have limitations, even happiness; otherwise it can produce misfortune. People who are prosperous live with the delusion that prosperity is perpetual: wealth clouds their minds and they cannot see clearly. But if their attitudes and ways of living are correct, then their good fortune can continue.

The Symbol indicates that those who get this hexagram can be successful as musicians or in the theater or entertainment business. Religious undertakings will also be advantageous during this time.

THE JUDGMENT

Happiness. It is of benefit to build up the country (or business),
And send the army forth.

THE SYMBOL

Thunder arising from the earth symbolizes Happiness.
The ancient kings composed music to honor virtue,
Offering it to God and the spirits of their ancestors.

THE LINES

Six at the bottom: Happiness that shows itself off brings misfortune.

One will be fearful, meeting obstacles and gossip. At work, what seems a good opportunity may lead to failure. But students and scholars will gain sudden recognition.

Six in the second place: Firm and stable like a rock. Do not wait a whole day. Continuing brings good fortune.

This line indicates that one will gain great benefit: students in particular will achieve recognition. A decision whether to plunge in or remain aloof should be made rapidly.

Six in the third place: Looking upward leads to remorse. Delay brings regret.

A time of sudden progress and sudden setbacks. People will not lead peaceful lives. They will encounter gossip and find that they cannot realize their plans. Stability cannot be found in one's work: a person may be suddenly promoted or set back. The student is in danger of failing to make a decision.

Nine in the fourth place: The source of happiness. One

receives great gain without hesitation. Your friends are already successful.

You can expect profit from your undertakings. Those employed will gain success and recognition, while students and the unemployed are likely to find jobs.

Six in the fifth place: Long illness, but still living.

You have many ideas and plans but cannot fulfill them. This is not the time for students and the unemployed to find opportunity. But an employed person may become successful by relying on some-one important.

If you get this line, watch out for sickness in the stomach.

Six at the top: Deluded happiness. Change after completion. No blame.

Arrogance causes conflicts and lawsuits, bribery in one's job leads to demotion, errors and ignorance in one's studies lead to slander. But if people correct their mistakes, they can avoid further mis-fortune.

17. *Sui / Following*

Chen, the lower trigram, stands for thunder, the eldest son, or an adult young man. The upper trigram, *Tui,* is beauty, autumn, the youngest daughter. The hexagram *Sui* portrays a strong young man running after a pretty girl. He impresses her, and they are happy together.

Those who get this hexagram are likely to be in a beneficial situa-tion. This contains the possibility, however, of an imminent decline. *Tui,* the upper trigram, represents the dusk of the day, a beautiful time aglow with the bright colors of the sunset, but when night steadily approaches. *Sui* also depicts the thunder (*Chen*) that grows weaker in autumn (*Tui*), or the autumn leaves whose beauty will soon wither, die, and be trampled in the earth. A person should conserve his energy: too much excitement brings bad fortune. Perhaps he should retire or return home. A marriage will be transformed. Friends will be gained and lost easily. Avoid new entanglements.

The Symbol is sometimes important in prediction. In 1970, the hexagram for the month of August on my horoscope chart was *Sui*. Just as it says in the Symbol, at the end of August I retired from my position at the United Nations.

THE JUDGMENT
Following. Great Success.
It is of benefit to continue. No blame.

THE SYMBOL
Thunder in the lake symbolizes Following.
In the evening, the superior man rests
And relaxes in his home.

THE LINES
Nine at the bottom: One's position is changing. To continue brings good fortune. Both friends and business are gained by going out. Success.

This line indicates benefit; those with jobs will receive promotions, while students will have opportunities for advancement.

Six in the second place: By staying with the boy, you lose the strong man.

If you get this line, you are liable to find yourself restless, detained, or entangled in gossip. If you are employed, you should consider resigning and awaiting an opportunity for a new undertaking.

Six in the third place: By staying with the strong man, you lose the boy. Through following, one will gain what one seeks. To continue benefits.

You will gain from your undertakings if you act correctly. For those with jobs, a high position through another's recommendation is in store. The academic will receive recognition through a recommendation.

Nine in the fourth place: Success is gained by following. But to continue brings misfortune. Going the correct way leads to glory (brightness). How can there be blame?

Expect the aid of an influential person, which will change misfortune to good fortune. If you work, this means you will hold an important position and succeed in what you set out to do.

Nine in the fifth place: There is confidence in goodness. Good fortune.

One will have the good fortune of plans that meet with success. The employee can expect to be promoted and the student can expect a position through a recommendation.

Six at the top: Deeply involved with one's fellows, one tries to continue. The King offers the Western Mountain.

People should be on guard against entanglements and loss, otherwise they will be subject to worry, illness, and general poor health. The employed person should guard against being slandered, and the student or scholar should avoid being insulted.

18. *Ku / Work after Spoiling*

This hexagram implies that, although conditions are bad now, improvement can be expected. The wind, *Sun,* the lower trigram, blows at the foot of the mountain, *Ken,* the upper trigram, destroying the trees, bushes, and grass. Later, however, the trees will bud and the grass will sprout: the land will again be cultivated. Thus the superior man, who provides moral leadership, chastises a corrupt society, telling the people to change and control themselves: society is once again put in order. Work after Spoiling represents a time of renewal and repair, new situations and prosperity.

If you get this hexagram and the situation is bad, do not worry. Try to change your attitude and rid yourself of bad habits; you can change your condition from bad to good. But after achieving success, you should withdraw. This prolongs good fortune.

For business *Ku* indicates a bad situation: organization or management is in poor condition, and financial circumstances are not good. One can do nothing about the financial situation, but he should try to reorganize the business. Then when more favorable conditions arrive, he will be prosperous again.

For government or politics Work after Spoiling means that the political party should reorganize itself and allow new elements to assume leadership. A new leader can change policies and bring improvement for all.

In romance and marital affairs a complicated situation is indicated. *Ken,* the upper primary trigram, is the youngest son, while *Sun,* the lower, is the oldest daughter: a young man will love an older woman. The upper nuclear trigram is *Chen,* the eldest son, while the lower is *Tui,* the youngest daughter: an older man involved with a young girl. In both cases marriage will be difficult because of differing temperaments and life-styles; even though they love each other deeply, they will always conflict. There can be no happiness in their union.

THE JUDGMENT
Work after spoiling. Great success.
It is of benefit to cross the great water.
Before starting, three days.
After starting, three days.

THE SYMBOL
Wind blowing around the foot of the mountain
Symbolizes Work after Spoiling
The superior man encourages people
To cultivate virtue.

THE LINES

Six at the bottom: If the mistakes of the father are corrected by the son, no blame. There is danger, but in the end, good fortune.

With the help of their families' influence, people will achieve their goals. Those who work will obtain important positions and introduce new policies.

Nine in the second place: In correcting the mistakes of the mother, one must not be too persistent.

This line indicates success, but you should not think of following in your parents' careers. If you are already working, you need not worry about losing your job. If you are a woman, your diligence and thrift will help you become rich and have a rewarding career.

Nine in the third place: In correcting the mistakes of the father, there is slight remorse. No great blame.

Overambition at work causes error, and hasty actions in school lead to trouble. But correct action will avoid disaster.

Six in the fourth place: Continuing to tolerate the mistakes of the father brings humiliation.

Although a person now enjoys good fortune, he will suffer a loss because of pride. At work one may be criticized for incompetence; the academic may ruin his career through laziness. Then there will be sadness in everything.

Watch out for trouble in the feet.

Six in the fifth place: Correcting the mistakes of the father leads to recognition.

This is a time of good fortune. People will marry, have children, move to new homes, or start new careers. Workers and students will advance and gain recognition.

Nine at the top: By not serving kings and princes, one gains higher recognition.

People will remain in their original careers, although for some now is a good time to retire; students should await an opportunity for advancement. If birth time and zodiac symbols are favorable, chances are good that one will be helped by an important person to achieve success.

19. *Lin / Approach*

The Chinese word *Lin* means approaching someone or something, dealing with someone, or handling some affair. The upper trigram is *K'un*, the mother, and the lower trigram is *Tui*, the youngest daughter. The mother guides and advises the daughter in a kindly but firm manner; the girl should listen carefully and obey her mother's words, which result from her wisdom and experience. In ancient times this hexagram indicated the manner in which the king or officials approached their subjects: they were kind and generous and guided with wisdom and experience.

The two yang (unbroken) lines at the bottom of the hexagram indicate vitality, growth, hope for achievement: spring approaches and things are beginning to grow. This is a time of good fortune. When the eighth month comes, however, we can expect the approach of autumn, when everything will decline: a time of misfortune.

In June 1937 prediction concerning the Sino-Japanese situation referred to this hexagram, with no moving line. The Judgment says that there will be disaster in the eighth month; I concluded that in August war would break out. (When the *I Ching* was written, the Chinese eighth month was August.) The Sino-Japanese War began on August 13, 1937.

THE JUDGMENT

Approach. Great Success.

It is of benefit to continue.

When the eighth month arrives,
Then there will be misfortune.

THE SYMBOL

The earth above the lake symbolizes Approach.
The superior man's will for instruction has no limit.
He is boundless in his support and protection of the people.

THE LINES

Nine at the bottom: Approach with sincerity. To continue
brings good fortune.

Cooperation and intelligence at work will lead to a high promotion.
If still in school, you can expect to pass an exam and gain recognition. Whatever you do, you should approach a worthy person to help
you achieve your goal.

Nine in the second place: To approach with sincerity
brings good fortune. It is beneficial for everything.

Cheerfulness will bring benefits in your career. In your work you
are apt to help a good man avoid an evil one and thus may gain a
high position. A student can expect to advance without any trouble.

Six in the third place: Cheerful approach does not
benefit further. If one fears regret, no blame.

This is a time of sadness, worry, and bitterness. Do not engage in
gossip where you work. In school you are likely to be busy, but you
should refrain from flightiness and flattery.

Six in the fourth place: Complete approach brings no
blame.

One will be in harmony with society and achieve one's undertaking, but be careful in the beginning. Working people will get
help from their friends; the student will have a chance for glory.

Six in the fifth place: To approach with wisdom is
appropriate for a great duke. Good fortune.

People will achieve smoothly what they desire. Those employed will get high positions, the student can expect a good job.

Six at the top: Benevolent approach brings good fortune. No blame.

This line implies success and a tranquil life for the individual. If employed, one can expect to be asked to take an important job as an aide; if in school, one will get a degree.

20. *Kuan / Observation*

The upper trigram is *Sun*, wind, and the lower trigram is *K'un*, earth or dust: the wind blows the dust everywhere. Business or achievement must be found elsewhere. The northeast is indicated by the upper nuclear trigram, *Ken*, which also means mountain and standstill: the dust is blown to the mountain, where it settles at a high attitude. Be patient and wait for your business to grow; eventually you will be successful.

In Confucius's work *Ch'un Ch'iu*, he tells of the duke of the state of Chen in southwest China who called in a predictor at the birth of his son. This hexagram appeared, with the moving line in the fourth position. The prediction was that the young prince would go off to another place and be prosperous. After the son grew up he went to Ch'i state in the northeast, where he became a minister of the court. After several generations his descendants became the rulers of Ch'i.

Kuan indicates a suitable time for work, study, or religious activities. It is also favorable for learning the art of meditation. If you get this hexagram you should strive to be a more careful observer and planner. This includes studying your surroundings and the conduct of the people around you. It also includes self-examination.

THE JUDGMENT

Observation. The hand-washing ritual is completed,
But the sacrifice is still to come.
All done and looked upon with sincerity.

THE SYMBOL

The wind blowing over the earth symbolizes Observation.
The ancient kings visited their territories,
Observed the people, and gave instruction.

THE LINES

Six at the bottom: Childish observation. For inferior
people, no blame. For superior people, humiliation.

Although activity is accelerated, results are slow in coming; in
spite of skillful planning, there is still no success. Beware of betrayal
by someone whom you trusted. Difficult conditions are in store for the
employed person; the academic will find limited opportunity for
advancement.

Six in the second place: Observation through the cracks of
doors. Women benefit by perseverance.

Now is a better time for action than for quiet. Good fortune for a
woman, bad for a man. A person may feel incapable in his job, and
the student or scholar may have trouble writing. One feels suddenly
happy, then suddenly sad.

Six in the third place: Observation of the circumstances of
our lives determines whether to advance or retreat.

Everything should be done with caution; avoid difficulty. One
will both gain and lose. The employee will be promoted suddenly,
then demoted. The student will be involved in disputes.

Six in the fourth place: Observation of the glory of the
country. It is beneficial to exert influence as the guest of
the leader.

One will benefit by traveling on business; one might be an honored guest in another city or country. The employed person will get an important job working as a chief assistant. The student will pass his exams and gain recognition; he may get a fellowship for study or research, perhaps abroad.

Nine in the fifth place: Observation of ourselves. No blame for the superior man.

People can expect to achieve their business goals and receive benefits. For those employed, this means high positions and generous salaries, working for the good of society. Students can look forward to gaining valuable knowledge and winning their degrees.

Women will have children and the sick will recover.

Nine at the top: Observation of the lives of others. No blame for the superior man.

This is a time of discontent: obstacles will stand in the way of your plans. Employed people should consider resigning and working for themselves. Students and the unemployed will find it difficult to improve their situations.

But this is also a time for the sick to recover and women to give birth.

21. *Shih Ho / Chewing*

Shih Ho refers to many things: chewing, justice, quarreling, obstacles. *Li* (the upper trigram) means lightning and clarity, and *Chen* (the lower trigram) means thunder and movement. Thus a person with a clear mind and much energy is indicated. *Li* also means fire and *Chen* wood, and here they present the other meaning of fuel on the fire: people who quarrel because they are easily angered.

Hexagram 27 is shaped like an open mouth; *Shih Ho* resembles a mouth with something in it—the unbroken line in the fourth place. This may be words inside the mouth which must be spoken, indicating how quarrels begin. Or a piece of food may be the obstacle: one must chew forcefully in order to get nourishment. In this way *Shih Ho* indicates success through hard work. Those who get this hexagram will have trouble in the beginning. The first three lines indicate hard times, but then there is a breakthrough: the fourth and fifth lines are good fortune. When you have reached a certain point in your success, however, you should stop or change your activity: the sixth line is misfortune.

In marriage affairs, this hexagram points to a third person who comes between husband and wife. But patience will result in a happy ending.

THE JUDGMENT
Chewing: Success.
It benefits to administer justice.

THE SYMBOL
Thunder and lightning symbolize Chewing.
The ancient kings made the laws and clarified the penalties.

THE LINES
Nine at the bottom: His feet are put in the stocks. It will injure his toes. No blame.

Caution now can prevent such personal disaster as punishment, illness (perhaps rheumatism), losing one's job, or failing an exam.

Six in the second place: Biting the skin, his nose is cut. No blame.

At this time one will have trouble trying either to advance or move back. A person may meet with gossip, and there may also be sickness or injury for him or his family. At work the arrogance of others will be frustrating, and in school one should guard against being slandered and one can expect difficulty in passing exams.

Six in the third place: By chewing dried salt meat one gets poisoned. Small humiliation, but no blame.

Now it is difficult to succeed even in small things. Because of limited ability and knowledge, one is in danger of failing at work or being criticized in school.

A person should look for trouble or danger within his own group.

Nine in the fourth place: By chewing on dried gristle one gains golden arrows. Firmness and hard work benefit. Good fortune.

A time of benefits: recognition for the student, promotion for the employee, and profit for the businessman.

Six in the fifth place: By chewing the dried meat one gains gold. To continue is dangerous. No blame.

Business will be profitable. At work you will rid yourself of someone worthless. In school you can expect recognition. If sick, you will recover.

Nine at the top. His neck is put in the wooden collar. His ear is injured. Misfortune.

Beware of gossip, insults, conflicts, lawsuits. You may be in danger of losing your job. Be concerned also about trouble in the eyes and ears and poor circulation.

22. *Pi / Gracefulness (Decoration)*

This hexagram means gracefulness, decoration, and beauty. *Ken,* the upper trigram, denotes a mountain and the youngest son; the lower trigram, *Li,* is brightness, fire, sun, and the second daughter.

When the sun shines on the mountain in the evening, it lights up vividly the flowers and trees, valleys and cliffs, precious stones and metals, rendering them all even more beautiful than usual. This idea of resplendent beauty is also indicated by the young man, *Ken,* and the young woman, *Li,* who together make a comely pair: vivacious, elegantly dressed, full of energy.

Those who receive this hexagram should beware. Although the sun is illuminating the mountain in all its splendor, it is evening and nightfall is near. Ornamentation is pleasing but is neither essential nor real, merely expensive. The next hexagram indicates what it may lead to: Decay. Affairs should be attended to now, before darkness descends.

THE JUDGMENT

Gracefulness. Success.
Small undertakings benefit.

THE SYMBOL

Fire illuminates the base of the mountain
Symbolizing Gracefulness.
Thus the superior man clarifies ordinary affairs,
But does not judge lawsuits.

THE LINES

Nine at the bottom: He decorates his toes and leaves the carriage. He would rather walk.

Activity benefits, but stagnation does not. One may have to travel a great deal to make a living, meeting many difficulties and being separated from his family. Be wary lest you lose your job or be expelled from school.

Six in the second place: He decorates his beard.

Wait for a good opportunity and, with someone's help, you will achieve success easily. In work this means a promotion. In school your success in writing will lead to recognition by an influential person.

Nine in the third place: Decoration with moisture. If you continue, you will have good fortune.

With the help of others, the employed person will get a good position, the scholar will gain recognition, and people in general will achieve success. Gossip about you will not hurt.

Six in the fourth place: Simple decoration. A white horse comes as though flying. Not a robber, but a suitor.

During this time there will be happiness in the midst of sadness, and safety even in danger. One meets with loss or opposition at first, but will finally achieve harmony or gain. It is a time for single people to get married. But if birth time and zodiac symbol are not favorable, one will mourn.

Six in the fifth place: Decoration in hills and gardens. A small roll of silk. Humiliation, then good fortune.

Do not expect to be greatly successful, but to have good fortune in a small way. People with jobs can expect a raise and better working conditions; those without jobs will get them.

Nine at the top: Simple decoration. No blame.

One will be successful in a simple undertaking; a working man can expect to be promoted, a student to achieve his goal. But if birth time and zodiac symbol are unfavorable, one can expect a time of mourning.

23. *Po / Decay*

Decay, disintegration, and misfortune are all indicated by *Po*. The season it refers to is autumn, when vegetation is decaying. The upper trigram, *Ken,* is mountain, the lower trigram, *K'un,* is earth: one mountain standing alone on the earth is exposed to wind and rain and can be worn down by erosion and earthquakes. The shape of the hexagram resembles a building which has only its outside walls and roof. There is little to support it and nothing within. It will easily collapse.

Po is unfavorable in many respects. It refers to the late evening, from seven to nine, a time when people are resting. For business a period of no activity is indicated; at this time one should be careful, work hard, and wait for a more active period. Romantically, the hexagram portrays a man who has many girlfriends—five yin lines and one yang line. But if he is not careful he will soon lose his money, energy, and girlfriends, and finally will collapse. For a woman this is a time of trouble and gossip. But remember that winter is always followed by spring, and nighttime by the dawn: the next hexagram is *Fu*, Revival, but you must be patient and wait.

THE JUDGMENT

Decay. It is unfavorable
To undertake anything.

THE SYMBOL

The mountain stands on the earth,
Symbolizing Decay.
Those above should act with benevolence
Toward those below.
Then there will be peace and security.

THE LINES

Six at the bottom: The legs of the bed are rotting. If one continues despite this, misfortune.

This is a time of discord with relatives. One should also beware of trouble in the hands or feet. A person should wait for the proper time and opportunity for an undertaking in his work. If birth time and zodiac symbols are unfavorable, one is in danger of having poor health, losing property, and not being able to achieve anything.

However, this is a good time for constructing a building.

Six in the second place: The frame of the bed is rotting. If one continues despite this, misfortune.

People find it hard to carry out their plans because subordinates insult them and superiors are jealous. They should beware of demotion or dismissal. Students can expect difficulty in their projects.

Six in the third place: Falling apart. No blame.

Life tends now to be stagnant: it is hard to find a good friend, and there may be sadness caused by parents or spouse. But one has a chance to gain recognition because of a special skill; if employed, he may meet a great man.

Six in the fourth place: The entire bed rots, reaching the body. Misfortune.

One may meet danger, trouble, conflict, lawsuit, or other difficulty. Beware of harm or slander in your job. If in school, you will find it hard to win leniency.

Six in the fifth place: A string of fish. Favor comes through women of the palace. Everything is good fortune.

A time of success in one's undertakings and harmony with others; working people can expect a promotion to an important position. Women especially will receive money and good fortune. The academic will achieve high recognition.

Six at the top: A large fruit not eaten. The superior man acquires a carriage. The inferior man's house falls apart.

This is the time to observe laws and regulations carefully, and thus protect oneself from potential trouble. A businessman will achieve his undertaking (perhaps completing a new installation), but he should be wary of insult from subordinates. The workingman can now gain more power. For the student, recommendations, recognition, and good friends.

24. *Fu / Return (Revival)*

Return, or Revival, signifies a bad time becoming better. What seems cold, lonely, and desolate on the outside may be full of light and energy within. Such is the winter solstice: the weather is extremely cold and ice and snow are everywhere; but deep underground, warmth is beginning to grow and spread. The lower trigram (*Chen*), wood, here represents the roots within the earth (*K'un*), the upper trigram. The bottom yang line indicates energy, warmth, and strength; for the present it is low and inside, but gradually it will rise to the top, bringing prosperity. It too is like the winter, which slowly but steadily flows into spring, when trees and grass sprout anew, and blossoms and flowers appear.

Anyone receiving this hexagram should prepare for a great opportunity. If you are in business, watch carefully: even if business is slow now, it will soon improve. For first marriages this hexagram is not favorable, but it is for second marriages or reunions after separation. If money is owed to you, it will be repaid. Success, however, will not come immediately; you must prepare for it and not merely wait with empty hopes.

THE JUDGMENT
Return: success.
One goes out and comes back in without harm.
Friends arrive without blame.
Going to and fro is the way.
Returning on the seventh day.
It benefits one to go anywhere.

THE SYMBOL
Thunder in the earth symbolizes Return. Thus in ancient
   times

The kings closed the roads during the winter solstice.
Merchants and travelers ceased traveling,
And rulers would not visit their territories.

THE LINES

Nine at the bottom: Return from not far away. No remorse. Great good fortune.

This line indicates a time of profit from your undertakings. At work you can expect to hold a high position. Now is the time to be involved in cultural activities. If in school, you will pass your exams and gain recognition.

Six in the second place: Quiet return. Good fortune.

It benefits one to rely on an influential person. Even if one is in a dangerous position, he will be safe; if diseased, he will be cured; if fired or suspended, he will get his position back. But if birth time and zodiac symbols are unfavorable, a person may find that he has to resign.

Six in the third place: Frequent returns. Danger. No blame.

This is a period of changeable conditions. Although one tries for quick results, the way is slow. One has many doubts and mistakes, and his job may often change. The student, however, will receive honors.

Six in the fourth place: One walks among others but returns by oneself.

Now is the time to better yourself. You have the chance to recover your job, or, if in school, to gain recognition.

Six in the fifth place: Benevolent return. No remorse.

A person can expect to receive property, get a promotion at work, or win honors in school. But he may still mourn: he should watch the health of his father.

Six at the top: Confusing return. Misfortune, disaster. If there is a battle, there will be a great defeat. The ruler of the nation will meet disaster, and it will be unable to attack for ten years.

At this time quietness ensures good fortune, but action leads to misfortune. By being too stubborn, you are in danger of appearing wrong. Even if you are criticized at work and ordered to leave, you will remain. If in school, be prepared for insults and frustration.

25. *Wu Wang / The Unexpected (Innocence)*

Wu Wang indicates that everything should occur naturally, without ambition or design. One simply does what he should and does not calculate the result. It is much like plowing. The farmer plows in the spring even though he cannot predict how great the harvest will be in the autumn: storms, droughts, or floods may come. When he encounters trouble or difficulty, he must adapt to the conditions, not struggle against them. (See the fifth line.)

The upper trigram of *Wu Wang* is *Ch'ien*, which means heaven, father, or leader; the lower trigram, *Chen*, means thunder, strength, or eldest son. The season referred to is spring and the image is that of thunder under heaven: it is going to rain and you can neither help nor prevent it. The hexagram also indicates that the young man (*Chen*) should obey his father (*Ch'ien*) or follow the direction of a leader; this will result in good fortune.

Those who get this hexagram may face a great undertaking in the future.

THE JUDGMENT
The Unexpected: sublime success.
Benefit. Perseverance.

Someone acts incorrectly: misfortune.
No benefit for undertakings.

THE SYMBOL
Thunder rolls under heaven;
Everything is innocent.
The ancient kings cultivated virtue
And used the appropriate time
To nourish all beings.

THE LINES
Nine at the bottom: Innocent actions bring good fortune.

Profit for all. Harmony for the employee with those both above and below him. Recognition for the student or scholar.

Six in the second place: Do not count the harvest while planting, nor plow the field that lies in fallow. There is advantage in undertaking something.

People will gain fame, money, and property. Those with jobs will be promoted, and students will pass their exams without difficulty. Profit for merchants.

Six in the third place: An unexpected misfortune: the cow is tied up, and a passerby takes it. The passerby gains, the villagers are in trouble.

This is a time of good fortune for some: an employed person will be given an independent position as manager or foreman, a merchant will gain profit, and a farmer will increase his property and stock. But others may suffer illness, loss of money, or entanglement in gossip. A student will find it hard to gain recognition.

Nine in the fourth place: If one carries on, no blame.

People will retain their property without loss. Those with jobs will manage their careers well, and students and scholars will be happy with their positions.

Nine in the fifth place: For an unexpected illness, use no medicine. Good fortune will follow.

This line indicates success in your plans. If you avoid difficulty, you will have a good chance to advance. But even if you are entangled, the problem will resolve itself. It is a time to conceive children. The sick will recover quickly.

Nine at the top: Innocent action brings disaster. No advantage.

If one can adapt to the changing situation, he can avoid disaster. But if a person cannot handle his job he may lose it, and if a student does not know how to deal with society, he can expect to face humiliation.

26. *Ta Ch'u / Taming the Great Powers*

Taming the Great Powers means the storing of great internal strength, knowledge, and energy for a vast undertaking, and it implies a bright, successful future. The lower trigram, *Ch'ien*, and the upper nuclear trigram, *Chen*, together suggest strength and energy within, while *Ken*, the upper trigram, has the attribute of stillness, indicating that the strength and energy are in storage for later use. But in addition to these spiritual qualities, *Ken* means mountain, standing for storage of material wealth. For upon and within a mountain one finds wild animals, trees, plants, and precious metals. At the same time the mountain, being solid, has its own inner strength.

If you get this hexagram it indicates that you have a great deal of work to do. You will encounter difficulties, but you should endure to the end and not despair. If you meet troublesome or bad-tempered people, try to cultivate their friendship; later on they can help you.

Keep in mind that a farmer tames an unruly bull so that later it will pull a plow. If you want to get married but parents are opposing you, continue to try to win their approval; many people will help you and you will be successful in the end.

THE JUDGMENT
Taming the Great Powers.
Persistence benefits.
Not to eat at home is good fortune.
It is of benefit to cross the great water.

THE SYMBOL
Heaven within the mountain
Symbolizes Taming the Great Powers.
The wise man studies ancient knowledge
To improve his character.

THE LINES
Nine at the bottom: When one meets danger, it is better to stop.

Now it is best to remain quiet and inactive, for disaster may follow action. If employed you should consider resigning; if in school, wait for an opportunity.

Nine in the second place: The axletree separates from the wagon.

A time of retreat. You may succeed with the help of another, but be careful of your health and beware of losing something; at worst there may be disaster or gossip.

Nine in the third place: Good horses compete with each other. It is of benefit to continue working hard and to keep the chariot safe. It is of benefit to go somewhere.

People will find favor with a superior or get help from their friends. Through hard work they will achieve success. Those employed will get good jobs, while students will advance.

Six in the fourth place: The headboard restrains the young bull. Great good fortune.

If you receive this line, you can expect to be promoted, pass your exams, or receive property and animals.

Six in the fifth place: The boar has a tusk but is gelded. Good fortune.

People will have happiness, good fortune, and will achieve their goals. Employed people will be promoted, while students and scholars will gain high positions.

Nine at the top: One follows the way of heaven. Success.

One can expect success in everything he does. For an employee this means a high promotion through others' recommendation. For a student it means recognition.

27. *I / Nourishment*

In several ways Hexagram 27 suggests nourishment. The lower trigram, *Chen,* means wood and therefore trees, plants, herbs, and all the food and medicines derived from them. The upper trigram, *Ken,* means mountain, on which nourishing things grow. *Chen* is also thunder, and the thunder rolling around the foot of the mountain suggests that soon rain will fall, watering the earth. The hexagram itself portrays an open mouth, the broken lines representing the teeth. The attributes of the two primary trigrams—stillness for *Ken* and movement for *Chen*—correspond to the workings of the upper and lower jaws: the upper is still, the lower moves. If both jaws work well together, then a person can chew even very tough food and thus get more nourishment, just as one can achieve success and benefits through hard work. However, moderation in eating, as in other things, is necessary. The jaws functioning together also present an image of harmony in society.

In addition, *I* indicates the other function of the mouth, speech. Gossip and trouble can result from careless speech. The first, second, and third lines of the hexagram all point to misfortune, and even though the fourth and fifth lines are good, you should watch what you say and be careful of danger.

For a young man this hexagram means that he has the energy to strive to advance in society. For an old man it means rest and retirement; his energy has run out.

THE JUDGMENT
Nourishment. Continuing leads to good fortune.
Observe the providing of nourishment
And the food someone seeks for himself.

THE SYMBOL
Thunder rolling around the foot of the mountain
Is the symbol of Nourishment.
The superior man is cautious in his speech;
He restrains and regulates his eating and drinking.

THE LINES
Nine at the bottom: If you leave your divine tortoise and look at me with mouth drooling, there will be misfortune.

This line indicates possible disaster due to arrogance or conflict. One may encounter slander at work traceable to bribery, or one may be criticized in school for brazen behavior. A student, however, will still have a chance for a fellowship or scholarship.

Six in the second place: Seeking nourishment from the top, one strays from the path to the hill. To set forth leads to misfortune.

People will encounter both good and bad fortune. There may be gossip and poor health. Those employed must be cautious of being demoted. The student should be wary of being slandered.

Six in the third place: One turns away from nourishment. Continuing in this way brings misfortune: no action for ten years, no benefit or advantage.

Owing to misconduct there is a danger of encountering disaster, misfortune, or poor health. The employed person may face criticism and slander. The student risks the loss of his good reputation because of notoriety.

Six in the fourth place: Seeking nourishment from the top of the mountain brings good fortune. One stares like a starving tiger stalking its prey. No blame.

People will be helped by someone, leading to success in their goals. Those employed will have independent positions and be honored by their superiors; students and scholars will gain recognition. But if the time is unfavorable, one will be liable to criticism, gossip, or dismissal.

Six in the fifth place: One strays from the path. Remaining in the correct way brings good fortune. Don't cross the great water.

With another's help, one will succeed in his career and will achieve his goals. Students, however, will be able to find only menial positions.
A trip by airplane or ship is not recommended at this time.

Nine at the top. Seeking the source of nourishment. Danger, good fortune. It is of benefit to cross the great water.

Everything bodes good fortune. People will have continued success and glory. For those employed, a high position and good income; for the academic, great recognition.

28. *Ta Kuo / Great Excess*

Ta Kuo indicates something extraordinary or excessive. Both the lower and upper nuclear trigrams are *Ch'ien,* strength; repeated twice, it means very great strength. Owing to their inner fortitude, those who get this hexagram can face danger without fear. They have ability and are capable of great undertakings, but there is also a tendency to be arrogant and aggressive.

Tui, the upper trigram, means water, lake, and also broken; the lower trigram, *Sun,* means wood, tree, and soft. Together they present the image of trees under water: a flood. The lines of the hexagram portray a ridgepole, the highest beam supporting a roof. The two ends, however, are weak (the yin lines in the first and sixth positions), bent because they are unable to bear the weight. This situation indicates that one's ambitions are greater than his abilities.

If a businessman gets this hexagram, he is likely to be overexpanding his business and about to run short of money. He will also have disputes with his employees. For marriage affairs, this hexagram is unfavorable: it refers to an old man with a young girl, and a young man with an older woman. (See lines two and six.) Although they love each other deeply, they will not find happiness.

THE JUDGMENT
Great Excess. The ridgepole is crooked.
It benefits one to go anywhere. Success.

THE SYMBOL
The lake rising over the trees
Symbolizes Great Excess. The superior man,
When isolated, is undisturbed.
If he has to retreat from society,
He feels no regret.

THE LINES

Six at the bottom: To spread white rushes below leads to no blame.

At this time you have a chance to accumulate money through caution and economy. If a student, by diligently pursuing your studies, you can expect a good career. If you are employed, be assured that your position is secure. But if birth time and zodiac symbols are not favorable, there will be mourning.

Nine in the second place: The withered poplar tree sprouts new shoots. The old man marries a young wife. Everything is favorable.

One will marry, or if married, will have or adopt children; perhaps an older man and a young woman will be wed.

Although one loses his job, he can regain it, and a student, unhappy for a long time, will have a new opportunity for advancement. Organizations will increase their membership.

Nine in the third place: The ridgepole bends under pressure; misfortune.

During this time be cautious at work or in school. There is a danger of being set back.

Nine in the fourth place: The ridgepole is strengthened; good fortune. But something else may cause humiliation.

A yielding manner will avoid trouble. At work you can expect an important position; in school you will gain recognition. Expect to be involved in some form of construction.

Nine in the fifth place: A withered poplar blossoms. An old woman gains a young husband: No blame, no praise.

Sadness grows from excessive happiness. At this time people may experience difficulty in their undertakings; some may not be able to continue on their jobs, and students will find it hard to gain recognition.

One should expect trouble from an old woman.

Six at the top: One walks through the water and it goes over his head. Misfortune, no blame.

This line implies sadness and depression. If a person is employed, he should be careful not to arouse his employer's jealousy. For the student, however, six at the top means high recognition.

29. *K'an / Water*

This hexagram means danger, misfortune, or entanglement in a difficult situation. The trigram *K'an* means water; one yang line in the middle surrounded by two yin lines indicates its attribute, danger. Here *K'an* is both the upper and the lower trigram, which means there are many dangers in your environment. You should be both careful and patient; do not struggle with all the difficulties around you.

Those who receive this hexagram should beware of trickery or deceit and be on guard against burglary and robbery. During this time they may be injured or become involved in a serious dispute. They may have a problem with alcohol. For women the hexagram indicates a time of menstrual problems.

A young man who wishes to marry for the first time will have difficulties. A young couple will encounter trouble: both partners will take other lovers, or financial problems will prevent their marriage. The hexagram is favorable, however, in exceptional cases, such as remarriage or marriage later in life. For study or research it bodes well, especially for religious studies and writings.

THE JUDGMENT
Water doubled. (Danger.)

Sincerity leads to success (peacefulness)
In your heart (and mind).
You will succeed in your actions.

THE SYMBOL

Water flows unceasingly into the depths
Symbolizing Water doubled.
The superior man constantly preserves his virtue
And practices his task of education.

THE LINES

Six at the bottom: Water flows repeatedly. One falls
into the pit of water. Misfortune.

If you get this line, you should avoid excessive drinking. At work
you are in danger of being reproved or demoted; if in school, you
may be slandered or suspended. If you hold a high position, however, you may avoid danger.

Nine in the second place: There is danger in the abyss.
One should work for small gains only.

This is a time of achieving small tasks and gaining small successes.
If you are a student, you can expect to pass your exam and perhaps
even get a job. But if birth time and zodiac symbols are not favorable, you may experience personal difficulties or contract a stomach
disease.

Six in the third place: Water flows on and on. One is in
the pit of the abyss. Danger. Do not act.

This line indicates difficulties and conflicts. If you are working,
you should consider resigning; if you are in school, keep studying and
wait for an opportunity to show your proficiency.

Six in the fourth place: A jug of wine. Two bowls of
food should be put into an earthen container and passed
through the window. There is no blame in the end.

A time for meeting a friend or getting married. For a working person, a sales position is likely; and although a student will encounter obstacles, he has a chance to become an assistant.

This is also a time, however, when one may be in mourning.

Nine in the fifth place: The water does not overflow its bounds. The waves are calm. No blame.

People will achieve their goals smoothly and without endangering themselves. One now has a good chance to win a glamorous position in public relations, but even in a lesser job he will have success. A student can expect to get a minor job.

Six at the top: Tied with thick ropes, one is put in prison among thorn bushes. One cannot find the way for three years. Misfortune.

If you receive this line, avoid all entanglements, both physical and mental. Be cautious, or you will be detained.

Students can expect to pass their exams.

30. *Li / Fire*

Both the upper and lower trigrams are *Li:* fire, sun, glory, brightness. A flame is not stable; it is always in motion. The hexagram signifies external conditions which are constantly changing, and internally it means a mind that is never fixed on anything or a person who is short-tempered, explosive, and full of fire.

Fire is an important element in many ways. Our bodies convert food into calories, or units of heat, and if we do not have enough of them we weaken. Those who get this hexagram should remember that if fire is misused or uncontrolled, it can cause disaster. They have plenty of energy and sharp, penetrating minds: if they apply their abilities carefully they will be successful, but if they misuse them there will be trouble. The trigram *Li* also means the second or middle daughter, a young woman who is beautiful outside (the two yang lines) and devoted inside (the yin line). She is welcome in society, and if she uses her ability she will achieve success.

In romantic affairs *Li* indicates that both the man and the woman are very passionate, but if they hesitate and contemplate for too long they cannot marry. In summer the hexagram is favorable, but in autumn it means misfortune and decline.

THE JUDGMENT
Fire. It is of benefit to continue.
Success. To take care of the cow leads to good fortune.

THE SYMBOL
Doubled brightness symbolizes Fire.
A great man perpetuates the light
And illuminates the four corners of the universe.

THE LINES
Nine at the bottom: The footsteps are confused. If one is cautious, no blame.

Avoid breaking the law. By being cautious the employed person can do his work smoothly, not crudely. The student should avoid error which can expose him to insult.

Everyone should watch his steps so that he doesn't injure his feet.

Six in the second place: The yellow light of the sun indicates great good fortune.

This is a time of profit. Those employed will gain important positions; those in school will pass their exams and gain recognition.

Nine in the third place: Under the light of the setting sun, one sings without beating the pot, bemoaning one's old age. Misfortune.

Trouble arises from waning good fortune, from happiness comes sadness. If employed you might retire; if in school you should avoid insult. Danger and difficulty will come again and again: misfortune.

Nine in the fourth place: It comes abruptly; it burns up, dies, and is cast aside.

This line indicates that if one is arrogant, he can expect conflict with those both above and below him. Insolence in the student will lead to error. Beware of trouble arising from fighting or fire.

Six in the fifth place: A flood of tears, sighing, and sadness. Good fortune.

There may be suffering or mourning, but good fortune hides in misfortune. If you are a student or unemployed, you can expect difficulty in your undertakings. Do not expect recognition at this time. If you are employed, you are likely to resign, even if you have a high position.

Nine at the top: The king goes to fight. Victory. He kills the leader and captures the followers. No blame.

This is a lucky time. People will make profits, succeed in their careers, or do well in their exams. Undertakings now are favored. But if birth time and zodiac symbols are not favorable, one will be isolated.

31. *Hsien / Attraction (Stimulation)*

Hsien, Attraction, also means stimulation, affection, and sensitivity. The upper trigram, *Tui,* means joyous or young woman, and the lower trigram, *Ken,* strength or young man. The energetic young man and the beautiful young woman are strongly attracted to each other, the man pleasing the woman with his courteous, deferring manner. This hexagram is quite favorable for marriage. If two young people are well matched they should get married, for the Judgment advises: "To marry a girl is good fortune."

In business *Hsien* indicates harmony between employer and employee and that there is enough capital and energy to keep the business running smoothly. It is a good time to expand and open new branches, just as after marriage the couple will have children.

Not only the name of a hexagram but also the moving line gives a specific answer to a question. A student in one of my *I Ching* classes asked for a prediction about her boyfriend. They had been living together for several years, and she wanted to know whether or not he would marry her. She got this hexagram, with the moving line in the third position. I told her that he would not marry her. The lower trigram, *Ken* (young man), represented her boyfriend; it also means standstill. When the moving line changes from unbroken to broken the whole trigram becomes negative, indicating no sincerity on his part. The third line reads: "Stimulation in the thighs. If he insists on following, he will be humiliated." Both the text of the moving line and the shape of the hexagram are unfavorable. After the next class she told me that their relationship had worsened and they planned to separate.

THE JUDGMENT
Attraction. Success.
To continue is of benefit.
To marry a girl is good fortune.

THE SYMBOL
The lake on top of the mountain
Symbolizes Attraction.
With a humble manner
The superior man receives people.

THE LINES
Six at the bottom: Stimulation in the big toe.

If you get this line, you will plan an undertaking, but if it is planned hastily, it will be difficult to carry out. If you are working, you may get a new job in your department, changing from a slow-paced position to a more exciting one. The correct course is to wait patiently for the proper time for an undertaking.

Priests and monks can expect to travel far to preach.

Six in the second place: Stimulation in the calves of the legs. Misfortune. Stillness invites good fortune.

One tends to be hurried and busy, but good fortune lies in quietude rather than activity. Employed people will find good fortune in their present jobs; if they are sent to work in another place, misfortune will result. Students and scholars will not advance.

Nine in the third place: Stimulation in the thighs. If he insists on following, he will be humiliated.

This is the time to demonstrate intelligence. But at work one should still be wary of losing his present position, and although a student will pass his exams, he should not expect high grades.

Nine in the fourth place: To carry on reaps good fortune; remorse disappears. If his mind is not quiet and his thoughts go back and forth, only his friends will follow his ideas.

This line indiactes that a person's mind is constantly troubled and his ideas differ from those of his friends; thus only minor success is indicated. If one performs his duties competently, there will be a chance for promotion. A student, however, will find no recognition now and only small benefits.

Nine in the fifth place: Stimulation in the middle of the back. No remorse.

Conflict. Perhaps one's strong opinions at work will create discord. In school one can expect difficulty in carrying out his plans. Only small ventures will succeed.

Six at the top: Stimulation in the jaws and tongue.

If you are a student, the time is advantageous to enter a profession involving speech or commentary, such as the theater or journalism. If you work, you should be on guard against gossip and accusations.

32. *Heng / Duration*

Heng, Duration, continues the meaning of the preceding hexagram, *Hsien,* Attraction. The upper trigram, *Chen,* means eldest son, thunder, or hard wood; the lower trigram, *Sun,* means gentle, eldest daughter, or soft wood. Here they represent husband and wife in an enduring marriage. The married couple follows the example of the universe, in which the heavenly bodies possess duration: like the sun and moon they do not change their course.

In business this hexagram teaches perseverance. The fourth line says: "No birds in the field. For a long time one is out of place. How can one get birds?" Perseverance brings benefits and profits. If you are a student, you must continue to strive for knowledge and an academic degree.

THE JUDGMENT
Duration. Success. No blame.
It benefits to continue.
Going anywhere is advantageous.

THE SYMBOL
Thunder and wind symbolize Duration.
The superior man stands firm
Without changing direction.

THE LINES
Six at the bottom: One seeks duration too insistently; to continue this brings misfortune. Nothing is of benefit.

If a person fails to be reconciled to his position in society, he will be troubled by anxiety, never peaceful. At work one will be out of favor with his superior; at school one will lack good friends who can help him. A slower pace of living and more time given to reflection, however, can prevent a breakdown.

Nine in the second place: Remorse vanishes.

A stable situation is now possible. At work one can maintain his position and, with caution, avoid failure; in school one has a chance for recognition.

Nine in the third place: If he does not continue to improve his character, he will be disgraced. Continuing (not to improve) brings humiliation.

This is the time to be wary of insults, conflicts, and lawsuits. Inflexibility at work and misconduct in school will bring misfortune.

Nine in the fourth place: No birds in the field. For a long time one is out of place. How can one get birds?

If you receive this line, you should not expect success, even with heightened efforts. Rather, be wary of losing your present position.

Six in the fifth place: Firmly instilling duration in one's character is good fortune for a woman, but not for a man.

Your misconduct is liable to lead to criticism or insult. Don't flatter influential people at work, and refrain from trickery in school.

Six at the top: Continuous agitation means misfortune.

During this time small successes are within reach, but not large undertakings. It is a busy period for those who work: they should not expect peace but, rather, anxiety. For students, there may be scant recognition.

It is also a time when wives will be of little consolation to their husbands.

33. *Tun / Retreat (Withdrawal)*

The essential connotations of *Tun* are retreat, retirement, and resignation; in military strategy it means the withdrawal of forces. Its lesson is that you should not try to contest an opponent directly, bu rather, compromise, or, if conditions are adverse, retreat or go into seclusion. The upper trigram, *Ch'ien*, means old man or leader, and the lower trigram, *Ken*, mountain or stillness; together they portray an old man in seclusion in the mountains. Thus *Tun* signifies a favorable time for an older person to retire from work, or for a leader to withdraw.

In business, those who get this hexagram are liable to suffer losses; they should consider closing down now before too much money is lost. This is not a good time to begin a new enterprise. During this period, however, certain businesses will be successful, including theaters, restaurants, hotels, and entertainment businesses. The hexagram is not favorable for marriage.

The eminent scholar Chu Hsi (1130–1200), who lived during the Sung dynasty, at one time wished to impeach the powerful and notorious premier, Han Tuo Chou. Before submitting his impeachment demand to the emperor, however he consulted the *I Ching* and got this hexagram. As a result, Chu Hsi withdrew his demand, resigned from his official post, and devoted his life to teaching and writing. The nickname he took for himself was Tun Wong, which means literally "Old Master of Retreat." Chu Hsi later became known as the third sage of the Confucian school, after Confucius himself and Mencius.

THE JUDGMENT
Retreat. Success.
To persist in small matters is of benefit.

THE SYMBOL

The mountain beneath the sky
Symbolizes Retreat.
The superior man keeps his distance
From the inferior,
Not with anger, but with dignity.

THE LINES

Six at the bottom: The tail in retreat. (Someone closely
following.) Danger. No undertakings.

People will encounter difficulties in action; they should, rather,
maintain a peaceful demeanor and avoid disaster. Those employed
should consider retiring if they feel something harmful happening
to them. Students and scholars should continue their research, waiting
for the correct time for undertakings.

Six in the second place: If his will is strong, like yellow
oxhide, no one can dissuade him.

One can expect conflict with friends or relatives and insults from
subordinates, but one's own calm demeanor can prevent disaster.
Now is the time to seek a position involving writing, speaking, and
criticism, such as that of news commentator. The student will pass
his exams and receive a degree. Farmers will add to their livestock.

Nine in the third place: Retreat with entanglement is
dangerous and leads to illness. Take care of women and
subordinates. Good fortune.

A person may meet with sickness, danger, or threats, but he will
receive help from his wife or a new member of his family. Although
one desires success and achievement or favors from his superior, he
will encounter trouble instead. In school large projects cannot be
achieved.

Nine in the fourth place: Voluntary retreat is good
fortune for the superior man, but not for the inferior man.

Though you are helped by a woman or subordinate, trouble is coming. You should consider resigning to avoid danger. If you are in school, do not expect a great opportunity now.

Nine in the fifth place: Appropriate retreat. To continue brings good fortune.

This line bodes good fortune. Those who work can expect promotions to better positions. Those in school will receive help from influential people.

Nine at the top. Retreat after success. Everything is favorable.

People can expect benefits from their enterprises; they will gain property and have good fortune in every way. Those with jobs, however, may resign, while students should wait for a favorable time for an undertaking.

34. *Ta Chuang / Great Power*

Thunder (*Chen*) is in the sky (*Ch'ien*), representing great power. *Chen*, the upper trigram, also stands for a horse or a young man, while *Ch'ien*, the lower, signifies strength and movement; thus the hexagram also portrays a strong horse galloping with great force and speed or a young man with much energy and eager for action. Favorable conditions are likely to contribute to the young man's success, but if his efforts are too forceful or he overexerts himself, he will be the cause of disputes. The hexagram, however, suggests a way to ensure good fortune: when the strong lines are in yielding positions (second and fourth) there is good fortune, but when they are in strong positions (first and third) there is misfortune. Yielding and compromise are the answer.

Referring to marriage, the hexagram means that you should be patient and treat the opposite sex kindly. This brings success and harmony, but if you rush into marriage, you will experience failure.

THE JUDGMENT
Great Power. It is of benefit to continue.

THE SYMBOL
Thunder in the sky above
Symbolizes Great Power.
The superior man's conduct
Does not oppose the rules.

THE LINES
Nine at the bottom: Power in the toes. Actions lead to misfortune. This is true.

Decisive action now is liable to bring conflicts and lawsuits, humiliation and remorse. Gossiping or evil actions will bring insult for the employee, and if the student tries to advance by taking advantage of a situation, he will be humiliated.

One should be on guard against foot trouble.

Nine in the second place: Persistence brings good fortune. It (the second line) is in the center (the middle way).

This line implies that you will be able to achieve your goal. Working people can expect high promotions, while students will gain recognition.

Nine in the third place: The inferior man uses his power, while the superior man does not. The goat butts against a hedge, entangling its horns. To continue is dangerous.

The essence of the third line is disaster from which escape will be difficult. Watch out for troubles, obstacles, conflicts, lawsuits; this may also be a time of punishment or mourning.

Nine in the fourth place: Persistence brings good fortune and remorse vanishes. The hedge opens and entanglements vanish. Powerful as the axle of the big cart.

Activity will follow a long quiet period, bringing good fortune for the individual. Unemployed people will get jobs, and students will succeed in their projects and pass their exams with high grades.

Six in the fifth place: He carelessly loses the goat. No remorse.

One is not able to achieve one's plans; no benefit. A serious time for the sick. One should overcome his cowardice at work to avoid failure. In school the student should not expect recognition now.

Six at the top: A goat butts against the hedge. It cannot advance or retreat; nothing furthers. If one continues to work through the difficulty, there is good fortune.

If you get this line, cease all arrogant behavior, otherwise it will cause you trouble. You may lose your position at work or encounter difficulties in school. You may be entangled in conflicts and lawsuits.

35. *Chin / Progress*

The two trigrams of *Chin* depict the sun (*Li*) rising above the earth (*K'un*) at dawn, a time of beginnings. The bright sun stands for all that holds promise or hope for the future, such as a new business or a young man. For business this hexagram means increase and growth: your enterprise can reach a high level of success, as the sun ascends brightly at noon. It is also favorable for anyone seeking a job. If already employed, you will be promoted, perhaps to manager of a new branch.

Chin also indicates a separation from relatives and friends, perhaps even leaving your homeland. After this period of separation, however, you will be reunited with those you left. *Chin* is favorable for marriage and establishing a new home and family.

In certain cases the hexagram is not favorable. When your business expands rapidly, you will be rushed and trouble will develop. The phrase in the sixth line, "to chastise his own city," indicates a dispute within a company, political party, or social group: the leader will argue with members or employees. The line also indicates, however, that dealing with these problems carefully and patiently will bring good fortune.

THE JUDGMENT

The Marquis K'ang (rich, powerful, healthy)
Is bestowed with many horses by the king,
Who receives him three times in a single day.

THE SYMBOL

The sun rising above the earth
Is the symbol of Progress.
Thus the superior man brightens his character.

THE LINES

Six at the bottom: When progress meets obstruction, persistence brings good fortune. If one lacks the trust of others, one should remain benevolent. No blame.

This is a time of both happiness and sadness. Lead a quiet life, for misfortune will follow an undertaking. At work one should look out for slander. In school, if one fails to win the confidence of his mentor, he will not achieve his goals.

At this time a person should not expect the trust of his neighbor.

Six in the second place: When progress comes with sadness, persistence brings good fortune. He receives good fortune from the Queen Mother.

The second line suggests that a man can expect help from his mother and benefit from his wife in achieving his goals. It also indicates that people will work under wise supervisors, and that students, though frustrated in the beginning, will find harmony later.

Six in the third place: When the majority assents, remorse vanishes.

People can expect help from their friends to achieve their goals. Those employed will be promoted, and students will gain recognition and find jobs. But if birth time and zodiac symbols are unfavorable, one should expect loss and mourning.

Six in the fourth place: When progress is like a hamster, to continue brings danger.

A time of conflicts and lawsuits. At work take care to avoid difficulties due to slander. This is not the time for a student to seek a job.

Nine in the fifth place: Remorse vanishes. One should not mind gain or loss. To act brings good fortune and benefit in everything.

A person who receives this line will profit from his undertakings. If he has a job he can expect a promotion; if he is in school he will win recognition.

Six at the top: Progressing to the horns. It is only in order to chastise his own city. Awareness of danger brings fortune and no blame. To continue brings humiliation.

At this time you can expect your income to increase. Students will find jobs, but no recognition. You may become involved in building or repairing a house.

If birth time and zodiac symbols are not favorable, there will be conflict or fighting.

36. Ming I / Darkening of the Light (The Darkened Light)

In this hexagram the earth, *K'un*, is above the sun, *Li*, meaning that it is night and darkness is everywhere. This is a time to restore your energy and wait patiently for the dawn. It is also a period of evil conditions.

If you get this hexagram, you should be patient even in the midst of danger. It is a dark time and you should hide your wisdom; even if you have ability or knowledge, nobody will recognize it. Activity now will cause you difficulty or make others jealous. You should expand your knowledge through study and research, and when the right time (dawn) comes you will be successful. *Ming I* bodes ill for legal marriages, but it is favorable for love affairs and common-law unions.

I can personally testify to the timeliness of this hexagram's advice. According to my astrological chart, *Ming I* is the ruler of my life from age forty to eight-one. Just as it indicates, while I was working in the United Nations headquarters and teaching and lecturing, many of my colleagues were envious of my knowledge. But after I retired and devoted most of my time to writing and study, I became successful as an author. In 1972 I completed a project never before attempted by anyone: computerizing the *I Ching* for horoscopes.

THE JUDGMENT
Darkening of the Light.
It benefits one to carry on
Through hard times.

THE SYMBOL
The sun sinking under the earth

Symbolizes the Darkening of the Light.
In approaching the people the superior man veils his
   brightness,
Yet still has glory.

THE LINES

Nine at the bottom: The darkened light flies and droops
its wings. The superior man fasts for three days during
his wanderings. His host speaks of him with derision. He
leaves to go someplace.

This is a mixed time: one should beware of disaster, of being
injured in the foot or hand, or of being harmed by a bad leader; but
one can also expect honor or a promotion at work—perhaps to the
position of an important assistant—and recognition. A student will
pass his exams in school. If birth time and zodiac symbols are favorable, one may receive a car or a horse.

Six in the second place: The darkened light injures his
left thigh, but he is saved by a strong horse. Good fortune.

If you get this line, you are likely to move up to a powerful position at work; if still in school, you can gain great recognition by
passing your exams.

Nine in the third place: The southern expedition of the
darkened light captures the leader. Act without rushing.
Continue.

Conflict is indicated by nine in the third place. A person may
travel to a remote place in his work, while a student can expect
sadness and anger. One should beware of trouble in the hands.

Six in the fourth place: He penetrates the left belly (an
inner place) and wins the heart (confidence) of the
darkened light. Then he gets the chance to fly away from
the courtyard.

People can expect to succeed with the help of others. Those who
are working may be transferred to another place; those who are

isolated will gain success and recognition. Women are likely to bear sons. But if birth time and zodiac symbols are unfavorable, one should look out for trouble in the stomach.

Six in the fifth place: The darkened light of Prince Chi. Continuance benefits.

This is a time of difficulty both for oneself and for one's family, but success will not be found in another place or country. Being thrifty, however, will help working people avoid difficult conditions. Both students and the unemployed should not expect to meet a good friend now.

Six at the top: Not light, but shadows. First he ascended to the sky, and later plunged into the earth.

After initial success, one should expect obstacles. At work one should beware of being reproached and losing his job; in school one must beware of failure. Aged persons should take care of their health.

37. *Chia Jen / The Family*

Chia Jen represents the family, and it indicates a time for the members to be mindful of their responsibilities to each other. In ancient China the family was highly organized, a small, self-contained society in which each member had special duties. The husband took care of external matters, working in the community. The wife, however, was even more important, for her charge was running the household, the internal affairs.

This family is indicated by the hexagram in several ways. The two primary trigrams are *Sun* and *Li*, the eldest and middle daughters, demonstrating the importance of women in the family. *Li* is also fire, and the woman (*Sun*) kept watch over the household fire so that it would not go out. In addition, each line represents a member of the family: the yang lines are male members, the yin lines female members.

The hexagram advises you to cooperate with the other members of your family. In addition you should coordinate with others in the social organizations you belong to, and in your work apply yourself conscientiously with your colleagues to achieve a common goal.

For marriage *Chia Jen* indicates success. The husbands (lines three and five) are strong lines in strong positions, and the wives (lines two and four) are yielding lines in yielding positions. This is a time of harmonious, child-producing marriages.

THE JUDGMENT
The Family. A woman's perseverance benefits.

THE SYMBOL
The wind coming out of the fire
Symbolizes the Family.
The speech of the superior man
Should have substance,
And his conduct be enduring.

THE LINES
Nine at the bottom: He sets up a rule for his family. Remorse disappears.

People can expect success in their plans. Those employed will receive good promotions or get important jobs; students and scholars will do well in their work or examinations. The single person is likely to get married.

Six in the second place: Her duties are to keep the household and prepare the food; she should not pursue her fancies. Persistence leads to good fortune.

During this time people will enjoy success and an increase in their property. At work one can expect to be honored and receive an important post. In school one is likely to win a scholarship.

Nine in the third place: If the members of the family are severe toward each other, there will be seriousness but good fortune. When women and children are silly, there will be regret in the end.

Avoid moodiness and bad habits. If you work, be conscientious and generous; if in school, do not become involved in a mediocre project, for it will not succeed.

Six in the fourth place: One makes the family prosperous. Great good fortune.

This is a time to expect an increase in income and a promotion. If you are still in school, you will gain recognition. Even if you are lonely now, you will become popular.

Nine in the fifth place: The king extends his love to the family (country) without worry. Good fortune.

Many people will receive help from influential benefactors. At work one can expect to be promoted and recognized. There may be an occasion for mourning, however.

Nine at the top: Sincerity and dignity bring good fortune.

You can expect to achieve your goals. An employee is apt to get a powerful and important post, and a student will gain recognition. At this time women are likely to rise in stature in society.

38. K'uei / Opposition

Hexagram 38 means opposition, fighting, or contradiction. The upper primary trigram is *Li* (fire), while the lower primary trigram is *Tui* (lake, water, metal). According to their natures, fire burns upward, water flows downward; fire evaporates water, water puts out fire. They oppose each other and cannot exist together. The nuclear trigrams present this same situation: *K'an* (water) and *Li*. No harmony is to be found in *K'uei*.

Those receiving this hexagram will not get along with friends or family; their suspicions lead them to oppose and contradict others. They are always meeting the wrong people in society (see the first and third lines), or encountering the wrong things in life (first and top lines). If these things happen to you, you should change your attitude and treat others generously. Your change will turn misfortune into good fortune. (See the top line.)

The hexagram is not favorable for business. Even if conditions seem favorable, the time is not good for you. Maintain the present state of your business and do not expand; if you have a new plan, wait for a more favorable time before attempting it.

For marital affairs *K'uei* means that it is better to proceed cautiously and not rush into anything; under the present conditions you will have many disputes. In love affairs a triangle relationship of two women and one man is indicated by the upper nuclear trigram, *K'an*, a man, and the two women, *Li* and *Tui*, above and below him.

THE JUDGMENT
Opposition. In small things, good fortune.

THE SYMBOL
Fire above the lake
Symbolizes Opposition.
Living with the people,
The superior man distinguishes among them.

THE LINES
Nine at the bottom: Remorse vanishes. If one loses a horse, one should not look for it; it will return by itself. Even if one sees evil men, no blame.

This line indicates discord in the beginning but harmony later. After first losing, people will regain. One may be set back at work but a promotion will come later. An unemployed person, however, can expect to find a job now. A student will achieve his goals slowly, with little help from friends.

If birth time and zodiac symbols are not favorable, a city dweller's pet or a farmer's livestock will meet with disaster.

Nine in the second place: One meets his superior in an alley. No blame.

With the help of friends you can expect to carry out your undertakings successfully. The employed person, under a wise superior, will receive a promotion, and the student will pass his exams.

Six in the third place: When the ox stopped, the cart moved back. He sees a man whose hair and nose have been cut off. Misfortune in the beginning, good fortune later.

Confusion in the beginning but order later; people will meet obstacles in their undertakings, but they will find safety in spite of dangerous conditions. At work one should be cautious of gossip; in school, great recognition will come after difficulty. But if birth time and zodiac symbols are not favorable, one may be injured or have trouble with relatives.

Nine in the fourth place: Isolated owing to opposition, he meets a strong man and they associate sincerely. Even though there is danger, no blame.

Obstacles in the beginning, smoothness in the end; you will find safety even in a dangerous situation. Recommendations from friends will help the unemployed get jobs; the student will receive help from his professor. Unmarried people can expect to get married.

Six in the fifth place: Remorse vanishes. The member of the clan bites the skin. Going. No blame.

You are likely to benefit from your undertakings and from help received from friends. Those employed will get promoted, and students will pass their exams and gain recognition. The unmarried person is likely to get married. But if birth time and zodiac symbols are not favorable, you may not get along with friends and relatives, and there may even be injury and lawsuits.

Nine at the top: Isolated due to opposition, one sees a

dirty pig by the roadside, and many devils in a cart. First he draws the bow against him, then he puts it down. He is not a robber, he will propose marriage. If he meets the rainfall, there will be good fortune.

A loss in the beginning, but profits and benefits later. One should watch out for gossip, slander, and hate, especially at work. In school things will be confusing at first, but all will go smoothly later.

39. *Chien / Obstruction*

Chien implies difficulty or danger. Water (*K'an*, the upper trigram) is on the mountain (*Ken*, the lower), representing a waterfall which carries great force and can easily cause damage. The hexagram also represents a rapid, rocky stream which is difficult to cross. In ancient China the upper part of the Yangtze River, flowing from the mountainous region of Szechuan Province, represented great danger; even in modern times boats have been wrecked on the rocks. According to The Judgment, the southwest is a favorable place. This refers to *K'un*, the earth, or the plain. Here the river is less dangerous and of benefit to the people through its irrigation of the land and usefulness in navigation. *Ken*, the mountain, is the northeast referred to in the Judgment, that which does not benefit.

The period between winter and spring is also represented by the hexagram: *K'an* means winter, *Ken* early spring. It is a very cold period, and the danger of frostbite is indicated by the combination of *Ken*, which can also mean leg, and *K'an*, icy water. It is not a good time for movement but a time of waiting for the season to change. If you get this hexagram you should not undertake anything; if you must travel, the southeast is the favorable direction.

This is not a good time for marriage. A woman will be pursued by two men—*Ken* and *K'an*—and a man will have rivals.

THE JUDGMENT

Obstruction. The southwest is of benefit.
The northeast—no benefit.
It benefits one to visit a great man.
To continue brings good fortune.

THE SYMBOL

Water on the mountain
Symbolizes Obstruction.
The superior man reexamines himself
And improves his character.

THE LINES

Six at the bottom: Going leads to obstruction. Coming brings praise.

People should remain in their present positions. Those with jobs will receive rewards and honor, but promotion will come later. A student should wait for a more favorable time before undertaking a project.

Six in the second place: The kings' officer meets many obstructions. It is not his fault.

One is liable to encounter difficulty, danger, and obstacles and may also be troubled with poor health. Employed people should devote their time and abilities to their work. A student should not expect to find an opportunity to carry out his project.

Nine in the third place: Going leads to obstruction. Therefore he returns. He will be happy.

Caution will prevent loss or injury. If you work you can expect to be offered an important job; if in school you will pass your exam.
This is a good time to get married.

Six in the fourth place: Going leads to obstruction. Coming brings about unity.

Be wary of becoming entangled in conflicts and lawsuits, for they could create much trouble. If you continue to be diligent at work, you are likely to be promoted. If you are in school, you can expect to receive recognition and then a good job.

Nine in the fifth place: One meets great obstruction. Friends come.

You can expect help in your undertakings and good fortune in everything. Those who work will get better jobs, while students will either pass their exams or do advanced study.

Six at the top: Going leads to obstruction. Coming brings great events. Good fortune. It is beneficial to see a great man.

You are likely to progress with the help of a prominent person. An employed person will be of important assistance to a leader. Recognition is in store for the academic.

40. *Hsieh / Liberation*

Hsieh signifies deliverance or liberation from the obstruction represented by the preceding hexagram, *Chien*. The upper trigram, *Chen*, means thunder and spring; the lower trigram, *K'an*, water or ice and winter. Together they present the image of springtime, when the first thunder wakes creatures from hibernation, and the ice melts and water is free to flow again.

You can expect to be released from difficult conditions now or have complicated problems resolved. For business it is a time of expansion and growth, just as the trees and grass flourish in the spring. *Chen* is also the period from five to seven in the morning, when work is beginning: if you are looking for a job, you will find one easily. According to the Judgment, the southwest is the favorable direction; there you will get along well with people.

All of the lines of the hexagram are good fortune, except the third, which says, "To continue brings humiliation." This means that if you encounter difficulties or obstructions, it is best to leave the situation and take a trip; to continue in difficulty only worsens it. When you return, the trouble is likely to be resolved.

Hsieh is good for those about to be married but unfavorable for those already married.

THE JUDGMENT

Liberation. The southwest benefits.
If there is nothing for one where one has to go,
Then returning brings good fortune.
If there is something in a place where one can go,
Then going quickly leads to good fortune.

THE SYMBOL

Thunder and rain come,
Symbolizing Liberation.
The superior man forgives errors
And pardons criminals.

THE LINES

Six at the bottom: No blame.

If you receive this line you can expect success in your undertakings. Your abilities suit your present job and you have a good chance for promotion; if in school, you will pass an important test.

If you are single, marriage is likely now.

Nine in the second place: One catches three foxes in the field and gains a yellow (golden) arrow. To continue brings good fortune.

At this time working people are apt to get important positions, and students will continue to pass their exams. A person who owns property or a farm can now expect to increase it; in addition, he may go on a hunting expedition in a distant place.

Six in the third place: A man carries goods on his back and rides in a carriage—this invites robbers to come. To continue brings humiliation.

One should be cautious and protect himself from theft or lawsuits. At work one should watch out for criticism and loss of his job. Students should not be lulled into carelessness by high recognition: disaster may follow.

Nine in the fourth place: Loosen your big toe. When your friend comes, you can trust each other.

At this time one should be cautious about associating with criminals or evil people. For the employee these associations might lead to disaster. They could harm the character of a student.

Everyone should be on guard against personal loss.

Six in the fifth place: Only the superior man can liberate himself from entanglement. Good fortune. Thus the inferior man trusts him.

One can expect to make a profit, or, if a student, to gain recognition. What the working person does will have important consequences; he may be involved in exposing dishonest people.

At this time a patient will recover, and a lawsuit will be won.

Six at the top: A duke shoots a hawk on the high wall and catches it. Everything is beneficial.

Many will benefit from their careers and receive promotions. Success is in store for those in the military and distinguished recognition for those in the academic world.

Perhaps you will soon be involved in the repair of a building.

41. *Sun / Decrease*

This hexagram means decrease, reduction, or loss. The upper tri-gram is *Ken*, the mountain, at the foot of which is the lake, *Tui*, the lower trigram. The mountain slowly crumbles into the water. This means a decrease in income or loss of money or property. Perhaps a gift you give to someone will reduce your possessions. There is an-other side, however: if you give something away, very likely you will be rewarded. The third line implies that if you possess too much you will lose some of it, but if you are lacking, someone will give you what you need. Applied to love affairs, it means that a triangle relationship will be broken up and someone will be left alone.

During this period, business investments will yield little profit, but a recession or decline now means prosperity and increase later. For the present, reduce your expenses. It is a good time for academic study or research. It is also a favorable time for marriage, and those already married will live harmoniously.

THE JUDGMENT
Decrease with sincerity:
Great good fortune, no blame.
One may continue.
It is beneficial to go somewhere.
How can this (Decrease with sincerity) be done?
One may use two bamboo containers of grain for a sacrifice.

THE SYMBOL
The lake beside the mountain
Symbolizes Decrease.
The superior man curbs his indignation
And restricts his desires.

THE LINES

Nine at the bottom: To go quickly after the work is done brings no blame. One should consider how much the decrease will be.

If a person budgets skillfully now, he will gain a profit. One should expect to work for society rather than for himself. Students will pass their exams. Many will gain the approval of those over them.

If birth time and zodiac symbols are not favorable, however, one should be cautious of failure due to excessive drinking.

Nine in the second place: To continue is beneficial. Undertakings bring misfortune. Without decrease, without increase.

At this time any improvement or planning for the future is likely to be difficult. If a person is careful and keeps his normal attitude, he can expect to maintain his present position at work or in school, but not to advance.

Six in the third place: Three people walking together will lose one. When one walks alone, he will meet a friend.

This line indicates help from others. At work you can expect help from your colleagues; if in school, friends who share the same goal will help you achieve brilliant success.

Six in the third place also means that leaders of social and religious groups will gain more followers. Single people are likely to get married.

Six in the fourth place: If he decreases his sickness (or faults) quickly, he will be happy. No blame.

Sadness now will develop into happiness, and you can expect to profit. The unemployed will find work, patients will get better, and a person who meets disaster will escape it. Good fortune for the student or scholar.

Six in the fifth place: He is enriched by twenty tortoises and he cannot refuse. Great good fortune.

A time of great benefit. Those employed will obtain better assignments and gain the favor of their superiors; after passing their exams students will gain high recognition. But if birth time and zodiac symbols are not favorable, one will mourn.

Nine at the top: If one increases (gains) without anyone decreasing (losing), no blame. To continue brings good fortune. It is beneficial to go somewhere else; one will find a helper after leaving home.

This line signifies a fortunate situation in which help comes from an important person; undertakings will benefit. At work a person will gain his superior's favor and others' respect. Students and scholars can expect to fulfill their desires.

42. I / Increase

I is the opposite of the preceding hexagram, Decrease, and it signifies an increase in benefits or advantages. The upper trigram, *Sun*, is the wind and eldest daughter and also means grass, flowers, small shrubs, and woody plants; the lower trigram, *Chen*, in addition to thunder and eldest sun, means trees. Together *Sun* and *Chen* portray a richly foliated forest, or a vine curling around a tree, covering it with leaves and flowers. The vine is the wife who adorns her husband, the tree, and needs his height and support: together they produce children, increasing their family. *Chen* is also spring and *Sun* the period between spring and summer, times when flowers and trees bloom and crops grow for the benefit of humanity.

An active period in business can now be expected: most of the lines signify good fortune and prosperity. When your income increases, however, you should be generous (see the fifth line) and never try to take advantage of other people. According to the sixth line, if a rich man is miserly and refuses to share his wealth, he will be attacked.

It is a good time for marriage. Even if others advise against it, get married right away: don't hesitate!

THE JUDGMENT
Increase. It is of benefit to set forth.
It is of benefit to cross the great water.

THE SYMBOL
Wind and thunder symbolize Increase.
When the superior man discovers good,
He follows it.
When he has errors, he corrects them.

THE LINES
Nine at the bottom: It is beneficial to undertake a great enterprise. Sublime good fortune. No blame.

This is a time of making great plans and succeeding magnificently. For employed people there will be promotions, and for students, success in exams and the chance to become masters in their fields, receiving acclaim.

Six in the second place: Someone enriches him with twenty tortoises. He cannot refuse. Perpetual continuance brings good fortune. The king makes a presentation to God. Good fortune.

A person who receives this line can expect to benefit from his enterprises and gain good fortune. If employed, he will receive a promotion; if in school, recognition.

Six in the third place: He is enriched by unfortunate affairs. No blame, if you are sincere and moderate in your conduct, and report to the officials for the record.

A time of benefit. Working people can expect added responsibilities and great success. Students, after winning recognition, are likely to launch new careers.

Six in the fourth place: If you are moderate in your conduct, people will follow you. It is beneficial to be dependent or move to a new place.

A person who receives this line can expect an important task at work; if he succeeds, he will gain the favor of his superior. A student can expect recommendations from influential people. A person involved in a lawsuit will win it.

The time is now favorable for making repairs on property or for moving to a new location.

Nine in the fifth place: If you are sincere and benevolent in your heart, without consulting, there will be great good fortune. People will trust your benevolent character.

You will have many good opportunities and will benefit through your own efforts. An employed person can expect added responsibility and a wise superior; a student will gain recognition. Priests and monks will move into roles of leadership.

Nine at the top: He benefits no one. Someone will attack him. His mind is not consistent. Misfortune.

If you receive this line, beware of jealousy and hatred. At work watch out for bribery. In school take care that competition does not lead to your being insulted. Caution now can prevent punishment, loss, and injury.

43. *Kuai / Determination*

Kuai means determination, decision, or resolution. *Tui*, the lake, above *Ch'ien*, heaven, represents water which has risen to a high point and which can easily overflow or break through its barriers. Struggling against the flow of water will not prevent disaster, but channeling it will make it useful. So it is in life: you must decide how to deal with a situation before it reaches a dangerous point, or things will take their own course and overwhelm you.

This hexagram indicates a person who has an important position and ability but who tends to be arrogant, and thus is left alone. If he uses his ability in a good way, he can help society; if in an evil way, he can do a great deal of harm. The five yang lines mean that if he is a good man, people will support him; but if he is not, they will oust him.

In business *Kuai* means that you will be successful: *Tui* and *Ch'ien* both mean gold, and the two nuclear trigrams are also *Ch'ien*. But along with success will come troubles and disputes. It is true that the three *Ch'ien* trigrams represent a great amount of energy, but still one should avoid force: *Tui*, the upper trigram, also stands for the mouth, meaning that you should speak moderately. Explain and compromise.

The imbalance contained in the hexagram does not favor love affairs or marriage. Five yang lines and only one yin line mean that those married will argue constantly, and those not married will have many lovers but no harmony.

THE JUDGMENT

Determination. Someone is proud
In the king's court, and the king trusts him.
If one exposes the truth, danger.
It must be told to one's own people.
Using force does not benefit.
It does benefit to do something else.

THE SYMBOL

The lake ascends to heaven,
Symbolizing Determination.
The superior man distributes wealth below him,
Without displaying his favors.

THE LINES

Nine at the bottom: Power in toes moving forward. If one goes and lacks ability, he makes a mistake.

Arrogance can cause trouble. At work rudeness could lead to condemnation. If you are a student, do not try to take advantage of others or to rely on luck instead of hard work, otherwise you will have cause to regret.

Nine in the second place: A cry of warning. One arms at night against the unexpected without fear.

During this period you may encounter fear, sadness, or danger. Watch out for thievery and robbery. But you will be successful in your career; if in school or in the military, you will receive recognition.

Nine in the third place: To display too much strength in the face—misfortune. The superior man is determined. He walks alone through the rain. He gets wet. He is unhappy. No blame.

Good fortune for those who follow the correct way. Knowing the situation and dealing with it carefully bring peace; otherwise there will be conflicts and lawsuits.

At work one may meet with difficulty and even harm dealing with people of evil intentions. In school a student should cease complaining, for this creates disharmony.

Nine in the fourth place: He injures his thighs. He walks with difficulty. If he were to follow like a sheep, remorse would vanish. People will not believe his words when they hear them.

Beware of conflicts, lawsuits, or punishments and of skin, ear, or foot diseases. If you work, keep abreast of your job; if in school, you should expect your project to fail, but you may still gain recognition by passing your exams.

Nine in the fifth place: Clinging weeds. Determination is necessary. Taking the middle path. No blame.

This line indicates that people will achieve their undertakings, though not without difficulty. A student who is capable of only small undertakings will find it hard to get a job. If a person has a job, he should be cautious of evil people attempting to do him harm.

The patient will recover; a lawsuit will be won.

Six at the top: Without a cry. Misfortune in the end.

If you get this line you will have difficulty in a new undertaking; it is best to keep your original job. If in school, you should continue to study.

If birth time and zodiac symbols are unfavorable, there will be punishment, conflict with relatives, or entanglements through gossip.

44. *Kou / Encountering*

Kou signifies occasional or accidental meetings that lead to friendships. The hexagram also means that new situations will arise suddenly and unexpectedly.

The upper trigram, *Ch'ien,* stands for heaven and also an old or strong man; the lower trigram, *Sun,* means wind, eldest daughter, and penetration. The man meets a mature woman whose powers of penetration enable her to understand the needs of others; thus she knows how to handle men and deal with society. Marriage, however, is not favored by this hexagram. Five yang lines and one yin indicate a woman with many boyfriends: the wind blowing under heaven is fickle and whistles everywhere. But *Kou* is favorable for second marriages or for people who wish to live together. According to the sixth line, the relationship will reach a certain point and then devolve into embarrassment and humiliation; it is best to separate before discord sets in.

The hexagram is good for short-term and seasonal business; entertainment enterprises will also be profitable.

THE JUDGMENT
Encountering. The female is forceful.
One should not marry her.

THE SYMBOL

The wind under the sky
Symbolizes Encountering.
The ruler issues his directives,
Announcing them to the four corners (throughout his
  country).

THE LINES

Six at the bottom: The cart is held in check by a metal
brake. To continue (this) is good fortune. If one goes
somewhere, one meets misfortune. The lean pig that
wriggles does not go any farther.

Be on guard against a lawsuit, sickness, or sorrow. At work you
may face demotion; if in school, do not expect a chance to advance.
You may receive assistance, however, from an influential friend or
acquaintance.

This is a propitious time for a woman to give birth.

Nine in the second place: There is a fish in the kitchen.
No blame, but there is no benefit to the guest.

For many this is a time to expect benefits and assistance, and for
women it is a time of conceiving children. People who work may
receive awards or promotions. For students, however, it is not a good
period: they are liable to have few friends and no opportunity to
advance.

Nine in the third place: He loses skin on his thighs and
walks with difficulty. Danger. No great mistake.

A time of disaster and punishment. If you work, you should consider resigning; you may lose your present position in any case. If
you are a student, however, you can expect to pass your exams and
receive recognition.

Nine in the fourth place: No fish in the kitchen—that brings misfortune.

This line indicates gossip, conflicts, lawsuits. At work one should watch out for blame or loss of his job; in school beware of insults.

An old man's health may decline.

Nine in the fifth place: The melon lies under the medlar tree. The glory is hidden. Something (blessing) comes down down from heaven.

One will be helped by an important person, with surprising results! Women will conceive children; working people, showing great ability, will be given additional responsibilities; and students, showing much improvement, will gain recognition. But the old man's health will be poor.

Nine at the top: Encountering on the horns. Humiliation, but no mistake.

Undertakings now will be difficult: one will be more independent but will lack support. At work, one can expect to have a position such as chief assistant. For students, it is a time of success.

45. *Ts'ui / Gathering*

This hexagram depicts a large number of people gathering together joyously in celebration, such as at a party, a convention, or a place of worship. The upper trigram, *Tui*, the lake, is over *K'un*, the earth; the lake is where streams collect. *Ts'ui* is related to Hexagram 8, *Pi*, Union, which also represents water on the earth. That water, however, is free to go anywhere, while in *Ts'ui* water has limits: if the lake becomes too full and overflows, disaster may result. The Symbol relates how the superior man deals with this kind of unexpected situation: he keeps his forces prepared.

Ts'ui is a good hexagram for business: a large gathering of people means a good market for your product. But be prepared for the disorder and overexcitement that can result from a crowd as from the overflowing of the lake. Calmness will ensure your good fortune.

Marriage is favored now. But people who are living together only temporarily should beware; joy and happiness now mean sadness and regret later.

One of my students in *I Ching* class got this hexagram and asked me to interpret it for her. The moving lines were the first and sixth. "The lower trigram became *Chen*, the upper becomes *Ch'ien*," I said. "Both of these trigrams possess strength and movement. Something in your life has already changed." She told me that her boyfriend had married a Danish girl and gone to Denmark. Then she asked what the future of her relationship with this man would be, and I replied, "You will meet him again. First you will cry, then you will laugh."

THE JUDGMENT
Gathering. Success.
The king attends the temple.
It is of benefit to see the great man;
This leads to success. Continuance benefits.
Offering a great sacrifice leads to good fortune.
It benefits one to go somewhere.

THE SYMBOL
The lake on the earth symbolizes Gathering.
The superior man keeps his weapons prepared
To meet the unexpected.

THE LINES
Six at the bottom: In the beginning sincerity, later change.
Disorder and gathering alternate. If you cry out, after
grasping someone's hands you will smile again. No fear.
Go with no blame.

Caution is indicated. There will be misfortune in the beginning, good fortune later. This means difficult conditions for the student. The worker may lose his job. One may be falsely accused.

Six in the second place: If you are introduced to something—good fortune. No blame. If you are sincere, even a simple offering will be blessed.

You can expect to profit from your undertakings, and with the help of a good person your goals will come within reach. A recommendation will gain a promotion, for the employed person while the scholar will obtain a job through the aid of his superior.

Six in the third place: Gathering with deep sighs. No benefit for an undertaking. Go with no blame. Slight humiliation.

This is a time of discord in the family, harm to relatives, and poor health for old men. For students it is a stagnant period, but working people have a chance to get a position in another section or branch of the business.

Nine in the fourth place: Great good fortune. No blame. (But the position is not correct.)

Incorrect behavior breeds trouble. At work, avoid gossip and jealousy; perhaps you should give up some of your responsibilities or even resign. If you are a student, do not expect your project to succeed now.

Nine in the fifth place: If one has position, people will gather. No blame. If he does not have the trust of all, he should perpetuate his magnanimity. Remorse will vanish.

A time of disharmony with others and obstacles in one's undertakings. At work a lack of trust from others could lead to failure to achieve a goal. In school unethical behavior could prevent the completion of one's studies.

Six at the top: Lamentation and deep sighing, with tears from the eyes and dribbling from the nose. No blame.

Do not expect profit, recognition, or benefit now. At work it is a time of disturbances and little stability, in school a time of sadness and remorse.
Be careful now of your health.

46. *Sheng / Ascending*

The hexagram *Sheng* means ascending, promotion, or expansion. *K'un*, the earth, is above; *Sun*, wood, is below. *Sun* here represents the trees and grass, rooted in the earth, growing higher and higher. *Sun* also refers to late spring, a time of rapid growth.

According to this hexagram, businesses will prosper like the growing trees that blossom and then bear fruit. One's efforts should continue, however, despite success, and growth should occur gradually, not suddenly (see the fifth line). Also, one should not become arrogant or proud as business improves and expands; nor should one let these favorable conditions lead to carelessness, laziness, or overaggressiveness. Unless one is cautious, misfortune can easily arise from good fortune.

Sheng is favorable for marriage. If already married, you will have children. An older person should care for his health; moderate exercise is beneficial. If you are seeking more business or want to embark on a new undertaking, the south is a favorable direction and the help of an influential person will ensure your success. If you are an employee, you can expect a promotion soon.

THE JUDGMENT
Ascending. Great Success.

One should see a great man. Without fear.
An expedition to the south leads to good fortune.

THE SYMBOL
The wood grows in the earth, symbolizing Ascending.
The superior man devotes his virtue to building things up
From the small to the high and great.

THE LINES
Six at the bottom: Confident ascending. Great good
fortune.

Indications are that you will be able to achieve the goal of your
undertaking. Those employed will win promotions, and students will
receive recommendations and gain the positions they seek.

Nine in the second place: If you are sincere, a summer
offering is beneficial. No blame.

This line indicates good luck: the sick person will recover, the
employee will get promoted, and the student will gain recognition.
At this time one may enter religious work. But if birth time and
zodiac symbols are unfavorable, there will be mourning.

Nine in the third place: Ascending to a deserted city.

Many will succeed in their careers: the employed person will be
promoted or be asked to manage a large business, and the student
will win honors. But if birth time and zodiac symbols are unfavorable,
one is likely to mourn.

Six in the fourth place: The king makes an offering on
Mount Ch'i. Good fortune. No regret.

Now is the time to benefit from the mountains, rivers, and forests;
perhaps you should take a trip.

This line indicates a favorable period. At work you can expect a
promotion; if in school, you may be the honored guest of an important person. If you work in the field of religion, you will find
benefit in the ceremonies of worship.

But if birth time and zodiac symbols are not favorable, you may attend a funeral.

Six in the fifth place: Continuing brings good fortune. Ascend step by step.

People can expect to achieve their goals. The employed person will get a promotion. The academic is ensured of a fine career.

Six at the top: Ascending in ignorance, it is still beneficial to continue unceasingly.

Beware of uncontrolled desires, or you will suffer. If you work, you are likely to resign. If you are in school, the prospects are good that you will enter research.

If birth time and zodiac symbols are not favorable, it is likely that you will have poor health.

47. *K'un / Oppression*

The Chinese character for *K'un* depicts wood enclosed on all four sides. This indicates difficulty in growth or movement and obstructions everywhere. Thus the hexagram signifies difficulty, poverty, obstruction, or oppression. The upper trigram, *Tui*, means lake, quarrel, or something broken; the lower, *K'an*, means water, danger, or sadness. The water is at the bottom of the lake, which is drying up, and the fish, plants, and other animals are dying for lack of water.

K'un is one of the four danger hexagrams of the *I Ching*. All six lines indicate misfortune. But you need not lose heart; keep your head and deal cautiously with all situations. Chinese philosophy advises that when you encounter extreme difficulty, you should make a change; perhaps this means moving to another place or changing your career or business. Then things will improve: the sixth line says, "If he feels regret, then sets forth—good fortune."

The hexagram is not favorable for marriage. A young girl may form a relationship with a married man, and from this nothing good can come. The hexagram also warns that excessive use of liquor will cause sickness in the stomach. There will be good fortune for those who study or do research, and this is an especially good time for religious activities and study. But it is unfavorable for an old man; he should retire and live in seclusion.

THE JUDGMENT
Oppression. Success. Persistence.
Good fortune for the great man. No blame.
If one indicates with words only, no one will believe.

THE SYMBOL
The lake with no water
Symbolizes Oppression.
The superior man would give up his life
To achieve his purpose.

THE LINES
Six at the bottom: His bottom is oppressed by the bare
tree. He enters a dark valley. For three years, he sees no one.

This line indicates fear, sadness, or mourning. One should consider resigning or retiring. A student should wait for a better chance for his undertaking.

Nine in the second place: Oppressed by food and drink.
The man in the red ceremonial robe comes. It is beneficial
to sacrifice. It leads to misfortune to set forth. No blame.

If you get this line, you can expect to profit from your activities and receive the help of an influential person. If working, you will be promoted. If not working or a student, you will get a job, perhaps in the field of religion. If birth time and zodiac symbols are not

favorable, activity will lead to misfortune, but inactivity to good
fortune.

Six in the third place: The man is oppressed by stone.
He sits on thorns and thistles. When he enters his home,
his cannot find his wife. Misfortune.

One should be prepared to meet with insult or difficulty. If in
school, one will pass an exam, but there may be trouble with one's
spouse. If a person is now working, he may find a job in a big organization.

Nine in the fourth place: He comes slowly, oppressed in
a golden carriage. Embarrassment, but good results in the
end.

You will meet obstacles in your activities but will also escape a
dangerous situation. If you lose your job, you will probably find another with more power but also more frustration. A businessman can
expect to receive money or a car, but if it is a car, he will have
trouble with it. Students will pass their exams.

Nine in the fifth place: His nose and feet suffer
punishment, oppressed by the man in the red ceremonial
robe. Joy comes gradually. It is beneficial to sacrifice.

You can expect to meet difficulties and obstructions in the beginning, but success and benefits later on. If birth time and zodiac
symbols are not favorable, however, there will be punishment, conflict, or mourning.

Six at the top: Oppressed by vines, he moves uneasily and
says, "Movement brings regret." If he feels regret, then
sets forth—good fortune.

Caution prevents threats and sadness. For the employee, it averts
entanglements and punishment; for the academic, insult or demotion. The businessman will profit by a business trip.

48. *Ching / The Well*

The upper trigram of *Ching* is *K'an*, which means water, and the lower trigram is *Sun*, wood. In ancient times, wells were lined with wood to prevent mud from mixing with the water, and wooden buckets were used to draw out the water. *Sun* also means long cord; this was tied to the bucket to raise and lower it. Water can be either beneficial or harmful to society. If the water is clear and cold, people will like to drink it, but if the well is old and dilapidated, the water will be dirty and no one will draw from it. It is the same with a declining business or a man who is not trustworthy: people will avoid them.

The lines of this hexagram speak of an old muddy well that the people no longer use ("Even animals do not come to an old well."). But repairing the well makes the water clear again, and the people return to use it; the lines turn to good fortune. Thus if others avoid you or your business, work to improve yourself or to rebuild the company. Improvements will attract people and bring prosperity.

THE JUDGMENT

The Well. The city might be moved;
But not the well. It neither overflows nor runs dry.
People come and go, drawing from the well.
The rope nearly reaches the water, but not quite;
The jug breaks—misfortune.

THE SYMBOL

Water on wood symbolizes the Well.
The superior man inspires people to work diligently,
And advises them to help each other.

THE LINES

Six at the bottom: No one drinks from a muddy well. Even animals do not come to an old well.

A time of obstacles. If you work, you should consider changing jobs. If you are in school, do not expect recognition now. If birth time and zodiac symbols are unfavorable, you may have poor health.

Nine in the second place: The well is like a valley (it is collapsed). The fish can be seen. The jug is old and it leaks.

One should be cautious now to avoid disaster. Working people should consider a vacation in order to get away from a tense situation; students should study and await the proper time for an enterprise.

Nine in the third place: The well has been cleared, but still no one drinks from it. This is sorrowful for me (the well), for others might draw from it. If the king is enlightened, he will use it for the benefit of all.

Now is the best to keep your customary life-style and not attempt any new enterprise. You are not likely to have good working conditions on your job, but for now you should accept this. If a student, you will not find an opening out of school but should take the time to cultivate yourself. If birth time and zodiac symbols are unfavorable, the line warns of sadness and even disaster.

Six in the fourth place: The well is being rebuilt. No blame.

This line suggests that one may work as a farmer, repair his home, or prepare himself to make a living. At work the employee should voice to his superior his ideas for improving the business. In school one should study the classics while awaiting a job opportunity.

Nine in the fifth place: The water of the well is clear and cool. People drink from it.

People will succeed in their undertakings and profit from them. Those employed will have the ability and position to gain respect in society, while students will achieve success and recognition and have the chance to get a job.

Six at the top: The well is clean, without a cover, There is confidence that water can be drawn. Great good fortune.

Sufficient money will be available for your expenses and what you plan will be achieved. An employed person is blessed with ability and a good record; he will receive a high position. A scholar possesses ability and knowledge, and he will be recognized.

49. *Ko / Revolution*

Revolution is meant in the sense of reform, renewal, upheaval, or simply change. Both the primary and the nuclear trigrams present situations of conflict. The upper primary trigram is *Tui*, the lake or water, and also the youngest daughter, while the lower primary is *Li*, fire and the middle daughter. There is a fire in the lake, an impossible situation: either the fire will dry up the lake or the lake will put out the fire. *Tui* and *Li* also represent two girls living together who cannot get along and are always quarreling. *Ch'ien*, the upper nuclear trigram, here represents metal; the lower nuclear trigram is *Sun*, wood. According to the relationships among the Five Elements, metal destroys wood. Thus on both the inside and outside of *Ko* a change must be made. It is a time of revolution.

The hexagram indicates change in all sections of society. In politics it refers to the form of government, in business to the organization of personnel at all levels, and in marriage it may mean divorce or remarriage. An individual who receives the hexagram can expect a change in career or location.

When change of this kind is necessary, it should be undertaken carefully and with the utmost sincerity; then there will be a good chance of success.

THE JUDGMENT

Revolution. When the appropriate day comes,
The people will believe in it.
Great success. It is beneficial to continue.
Remorse vanishes.

THE SYMBOL

Within the lake, fire—
This symbolizes Revolution.
The superior man makes a calendar,
Clearly arranging the seasons.

THE LINES

Nine at the bottom: To strengthen it, use yellow oxhide.

If you receive this line, you should maintain your usual manner and not be overly ambitious or chase progress. At work you will be able to keep your position, but you should not seek promotion. If you are in school, prepare your studies carefully and do not depend on luck alone.

Six in the second place: When the right day for revolution arrives, start. Good fortune. No blame.

This line presages much good luck, with promotion for employed persons and recognition for students.

Nine in the third place: To advance leads to misfortune. To continue leads to danger. When the idea of revolution has been spoken publicly three times, the people will believe it.

A person can expect many disturbances. Carelessness at work may lead to disappointment and demotion. Failure in school means that one must try again.

Nine in the fourth place: Remorse vanishes. People believe him. Changing the government brings good fortune.

Nine in the fourth place indicates great good luck. The employed person will receive a promotion immediately. Many job opportunities will arise for the academic.

Nine in the fifth place: The great man transforms himself like a tiger. Even before prediction by the oracle, people will believe him.

A man can expect a job, a scholarship, a promotion, or a new enterprise. But a woman will have no good fortune.

Six at the top: The superior man transforms himself like a leopard. The inferior man changes his attitude. To advance leads to misfortune. To remain and persist leads to good fortune.

If people obey the law and preserve order, they can avoid trouble. Those without jobs can expect to get them, but those with jobs are likely to resign. Students who write beautifully will be recognized for their efforts.

50. *Ting / The Caldron*

The broken line at the bottom of *Ting* represents the legs of the caldron, the lower nuclear trigram, *Ch'ien*, is the metal out of which the caldron is made, the broken line in the middle of the upper trigram, *Li*, symbolizes the contents of the caldron, and the unbroken line at the top is the cover.

Ko, the preceding hexagram, means the removal of old material;

Ting is involved in its transformation. The symbol of *Ting* is fire above and wood below. *Sun,* the lower trigram, also means wind; it blows the fire and makes it hotter. The fire boils the water (*Tui,* the upper nuclear trigram), changing its form from liquid to steam and changing raw food into a well-cooked, edible meal. The burning wood is transformed into ashes.

Since a caldron is used to prepare food, this hexagram also has the meaning of nourishment. The three legs of the caldron symbolize the executive, judicial, and legislative branches of government, so the hexagram represents the governing power as well.

Those who receive this hexagram are destined to plan well in establishing a business. *Ting* also indicates a situation in which three people will be able to work in harmony. The top line indicates great success and good fortune.

THE JUDGMENT
The Caldron. Great good fortune. Success.

THE SYMBOL
Fire above wood symbolizes the Caldron.
The superior man makes his destiny firm
With a correct position.

THE LINES
Six at the bottom: A caldron overturned by its legs—it is beneficial to clean out the stagnating matter. One takes a concubine to get a son. No blame.

Happiness arises from sadness, and with the help of another, one will succeed. For working people this means promotion; after a failure for students it means an initial setback followed by recognition.

At this time a man may have a child by his mistress.

Nine in the second place: The caldron is filled with food. My associates are jealous, but they cannot harm me. Good fortune.

Even though a person profits from his business or performs his work carefully and well, he should still beware lest others harm or disturb him. At this time, a student will find it hard to get a position, though he has a good education.

Nine in the third place: The handles of the caldron are changed. Its activity will be obstructed. The fat of the pheasant is not eaten. Once the rain comes, regret vanishes. Good fortune in the end.

This line indicates difficulty in the beginning, but later success. Slander against you may deprive you of your job, but you will find another. If in school, you should expect obstacles now whatever you do. But for old people this is a time of good fortune, and for young people success is predicted.

Nine in the fourth place: The legs of the caldron are split. The duke's meal is spilled and his face turns red. Misfortune.

At this time a person is in danger of losing property or his job. If he does not already have a job, he will find it hard to get one. One should also beware of physical injury, especially in the feet. If birth time and zodiac symbols are not favorable, one is liable to have poor health.

Six in the fifth place: The caldron has yellow handles and golden carrying rings. Continuing brings advantage.

A time of benefit: working people will be successful and move up to important jobs, students will pass their exams and win recognition, farmers and other rural people will gain more land, and positions of leadership will be bestowed on the religious.

Nine at the top: The caldron has carrying rings of jade. Great good fortune. Benefit in everything.

You can expect to achieve your goals and find profit and security. Those without jobs will find them, and students, helped by recommendations, will find good opportunities. A working person should now consider retiring if he has advanced to that time of life.

If birth time and zodiac symbols are unfavorable, however, you should guard against poor health.

51. *Chen / Thunder (Shock)*

Both the upper and lower trigrams of Hexagram 51 are *Chen*—thunder, the eldest son, spring—thus the hexagram means thunder, arousing, threat, fear, or shaking. Great claps of thunder burst in the spring sky, waking creatures from their hibernation and causing fear and trembling. But after the thunder and the following rain have gone, the weather clears up again. It is the same in human affairs: Even after a great fright, fear will pass, and one will be able to laugh once more.

The two *Chen* trigrams also represent a young man who has twice the normal amount of strength and energy. Just as the thunder arouses creatures in the spring, so he is able to stir people to great undertakings. Too much strength and movement, however, indicate a need for restraint and moderation. One should learn to pause or there may be trouble or injury. Most of the lines of the hexagram point to danger, shock, or misfortune.

The hexagram *Chen* indicates benefit in a theater, broadcasting, sports, or military career, but be very cautious, or there may be injury. It is not favorable for a first marriage: either people will gossip about you or you will quarrel with your betrothed. The two arousings, however, mean that the hexagram is good for a second marriage. If you lose something, don't fret; you will regain it. Have no fear of a crowd or riot. It is a good time to begin an enterprise in a new place.

THE JUDGMENT

Thunder. Success.
Thunder comes—ho ho!
Speaking and laughing—ha ha!
It shocks and terrifies for a hundred miles.
But one does not drop the spoon or chalice.

THE SYMBOL
Thunder doubled symbolizes shock.
The superior man contemplates himself
With fear and caution.

THE LINES
Nine at the bottom: Thunder comes—ho ho! Later there
are smiles and happy words—ha ha! Good fortune.

You may be threatened at first, but you will find happiness and
good luck later. If in school, you can expect sudden recognition, perhaps leading to a job as a leader or manager.

Six in the second place: Thunder comes, causing danger.
You will lose a great deal of your wealth, then climb nine
hills without searching for it. After seven days you will
regain it.

At this time a person faces danger at work from gossip or intrigue.
In school there will be confusion at the beginning of a project but
success later. One should watch out for his health. Youths, however,
can be expected to show their customary bravado.

Six in the third place: Thunder comes, causing a terrified
manner. But if one is cautious, one remains free of disaster.

As the line says, if you are cautious you can avoid disaster. If not,
you can expect to be criticized at work for laziness and inability; in
school the problem will be neglect of your studies.

Nine in the fourth place: Thunder causes mire.

Even with a humble manner, a person can achieve nothing during
this time; at work or in school one can expect a setback. If birth time
and zodiac symbols are not favorable, one will be involved in trouble.

Six in the fifth place: Thunder going back and forth
brings danger. No great loss. Something remains to be
achieved.

If you are working now, you are secure in your present job; if in school, you will continue your studies. But still you have cause to worry: you may injure a foot or hand.

Six at the top: Thunder causes trembling and frightened looks. Undertaking—misfortune. It will not threaten your own body, but it might your neighbor. No blame.
There will be gossip about marriage.

By being careful and cautious, one will have good fortune. During this period a student should avoid dangerous, fearful, or sad situations; an employed person should beware of losing his job.

If birth time and zodiac symbols are not favorable, one's spouse and neighbors are liable to have trouble.

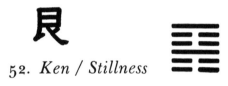

52. *Ken / Stillness*

Ken is another hexagram made up of the same two trigrams. The trigram *Ken* means mountain and its characteristic is stillness. Two mountains together strongly suggest immobility. Besides stillness the hexagram means stopping, restriction, and control.

This hexagram is related to both Taoist and Buddhist meditation. In fact, one Buddhist school derives its basic principles of meditation from two *I Ching* hexagrams: Observation (Hexagram 20) and *Ken*. *Ken* means stillness not only of the body but also of the mind.

Stillness is not permanent, however, for according to the philosophy of the *I Ching*, stillness grows out of movement (the preceding hexagram) and movement follows stillness (the next hexagram).

If you receive this hexagram you should observe the situation carefully and quietly devise a plan of action. In business it is a time to work on your own and not depend on others for help: you will build success gradually. If you are already married or living with someone, you will have harmony and peace for a long time, but if you do not have a partner it will not be easy to get along with the opposite sex.

THE JUDGMENT

Stillness. Keeping the back still—
One feels that the body no longer exists.
Even when one walks in the courtyard,
One sees no people. No blame.

THE SYMBOL

Mountain next to mountain
Symbolizes Stillness.
The superior man's thoughts
Do not go beyond his position.

THE LINES

Six at the bottom: Keeping the toes still. No error.
Continued persistence is advantageous.

You can expect to keep your present job or position without loss or trouble. For the student, however, the time is not good for undertaking anything.

Six in the second place: Keeping the calves still. But he cannot restrain the movements that follow, and he is uneasy in his mind.

A person cannot achieve his goal now. He suffers from fatigue, or has trouble with his family, or has difficulty with his feet; his mind is troubled constantly. At work a person lacks the ability to pull out of a bad period or depression, and in school one does not have any good opportunities now.

Nine in the third place: Keeping the loins and the middle of the spine still. Danger. His heart is like an anxious flame.

Arrogance leads to trouble and danger. If working, you can expect an important position in a remote place; if in school, you will gain recognition. But if birth time and zodiac symbols are not favorable, you or your famly should beware of sickness of the heart, eyes, or back. You may meet obstacles in your career or have family trouble.

Six in the fourth place: Keeping the body still. No error.

This is a bad time to be aggressive. You can keep your present position and life-style, but do not expect promotion or advancement.

Six in the fifth place: Keeping the jaws still. His speech has order. Remorse vanishes.

Many will achieve their undertakings, gain recognition, and be in harmony with others. It is a good time for one to seek an important position in society or government, working as a writer or commentator.

Old and young people, however, are liable to be troubled by indigestion during this time.

Nine at the top: Keeping still with benevolence. Good fortune.

A time of much good luck. You can expect to gain property, profit from a business, receive a promotion, or be recognized in school. You may also change jobs for the better.

53. *Chien / Gradual Development*

Chien, Gradual Development, implies improvement and gradual increase. The upper trigram is *Sun*, wood and eldest daughter; the lower is *Ken*, mountain and youngest son. Trees grow slowly on the mountain; the son and daughter grow up gradually. This idea is also expressed by the nuclear trigrams. *Li,* the upper, means a bird; in this case it is a goose that leaves the water (*K'an,* the lower nuclear trigram) and flies to the bank of the river, then to the mountain, thus gradually flying higher and higher.

A person who gets this hexagram will have good fortune if he proceeds with his plans step by step. The lines demonstrate the correct course. Even though there may be trouble along the way (as in the third line) success will come in the end (as in the sixth line).

The hexagram is on the whole favorable for love and upcoming marriage. *Sun* and *Ken* represent a young man and woman reaching marriageable age, and the goose which *Li* stands for is a traditional engagement present in China. Sometimes, however, it is the moving line that determines the prediction. A student in my *I Ching* class wanted to know her situation regarding marriage. She received this hexagram with a moving line in the third place—"The man sets out and does not return." She confirmed that her boyfriend had been away for three years and that she had not heard from him.

If you are already married and receive this hexagram, you should be wary of the involvement of another person in your marriage: the nuclear trigrams are *Li,* a woman, and *K'an,* a man.

THE JUDGMENT
Gradual Development. The marriage of a girl—
Good fortune. It benefits to continue.

THE SYMBOL
A tree on the mountain
Symbolizes Gradual Development.
The superior man, in maintaining his virtue,
Improve society's customs.

THE LINES
Six at the bottom: The wild goose gradually approaches the shore. The boy is in danger. There is gossip. No blame.

This line indicates difficulty, but you will ultimately be able to achieve your undertaking. The prospects are now good for finding work as a commentator, writer, lawyer, or consultant.

A student should not expect help in overcoming his obstacles.

Six in the second place: The wild goose gradually approaches a big rock. It eats and drinks joyfully. Good fortune.

Good fortune in everything and comfort everywhere. People will come into money and will eat well. Those employed will find better jobs, and students will pass their exams with honor.

Nine in the third place: The wild goose gradually approaches the highland. The man sets out and does not return. The woman is pregnant, but does not give birth. Misfortune. It is beneficial to protect oneself from robbers.

Fearfulness and disharmony are indicated by this line; at work one is in danger of losing his job, and in school progress will be slow. As the line says, "protect oneself from robbers."

Six in the fourth place: The wild goose gradually approaches the tree, seeking a safe branch. No blame.

This is a time of contentment in your personal life, without fear or sadness; but at work you should expect an unstable situation and difficulty in dealing with arrogant people. A student will pass his exams and begin a career.

You will benefit now by participating in the construction of a building.

Nine in the fifth place: The wild goose gradually approaches the top of the hill. The woman is not pregnant for three years. In the end, nothing can overcome her. Good fortune.

There will be confusion in the beginning, but understanding later; after overcoming obstacles, things will go smoothly in your life. Working people will encounter gossip. Those not working, including students, will find positions eventually. Old men and children, however, will suffer from poor health.

Nine at the top: The wild goose gradually approaches the cloudy heights. Its feathers can be used in ritual decoration. Good fortune.

You will carry out a significant undertaking with someone's help. Those employed will receive important responsibilities and be respected by society, while a student will gain unexpected success and recognition. Good fortune.

54. *Kuei Mei / The Marrying Girl*

Kuei Mei indicates marriage, fruition, or a final resolution. *Chen*, thunder and the eldest son, is the upper trigram, and *Tui*, lake, youngest daughter, and beauty, the lower. *Tui* here is a beautiful young girl with little experience who is swept off her feet by an older man. They love each other deeply, but they get married quickly without the appropriate procedures.

Although *Kuei Mei* represents marriage, it indicates little permanence. The upper nuclear trigram is *K'an*, water, and the lower is *Li*, the sun. The sun evaporates the water, which rises up to form clouds. Then thunder (*Chen*) heralds the rain, which floods the lake below (*Tui*) to overflowing: the water rises quickly and falls as swiftly. In the same way, the strong attraction between the older man and the young girl soon gives way to unfaithfulness, quarreling, and eventually misfortune—the top line. This is in accordance with Chinese philosophy, which holds that when events lead to an extreme state, they begin to evolve to the opposite.

In Confucius's book *Ch'un Ch'iu*, the story is told of the duke of the state of Chin, who, when making a prediction about his daughter's marriage to the Marquis of Ch'in, received this hexagram, with the moving line in the sixth place. He interpreted that the marriage would be unfavorable because fighting would break out between their two states. There was, in fact, prolonged warfare between them.

A person who receives this hexagram should be cautious in business matters and frugal in his personal life. Common-law marriages are favored.

THE JUDGMENT

The Marrying Girl. Undertaking leads to misfortune. Nothing benefits.

THE SYMBOL

Thunder above the lake
Symbolizes the Marrying Girl.
The superior man knows the cause of error,
And persists in his virtue to the end.

THE LINES

Nine at the bottom: The marrying girl is to be a concubine. A crippled man can walk. Undertaking is good fortune.

Even with limited ability a person will achieve his undertakings by depending on someone influential. One will perhaps gain recognition at work in a chief assistant's position; in school one can expect to pass his exams. One will also meet a boyfriend or girlfriend.

Nine in the second place: A one-eyed man can see. It benefits the solitary man to keep quiet.

If you get this line you can expect to maintain your present position without any trouble. This also means that you are not likely to be promoted, nor will students and unemployed persons have opportunities for advancement. If birth time and zodiac symbols are not favorable, you should be on guard against poor health.

Six in the third place: The marrying girl is to be a maidservant. She marries as a concubine.

Sudden advance, sudden retreat. One faces hard work, sadness and bitterness, perhaps divorce or the breakup of friendships, and the making of new friends. At work one should expect a setback, and students and the unemployed should wait for the right opportunity.

Nine in the fourth place: The marrying girl postpones marriage. She will marry later, waiting for the right time.

At this time you can expect to change jobs or to wait for one. If you are a merchant, you will find it advantageous to take a business trip.

This is not a good season for marriage: single people should wait for a more appropriate time.

Six in the fifth place: Emperor I gives his daughter in marriage. The embroidered dress of the princess is not as splendid as that of the concubine. The moon is nearly full. Good fortune.

You will achieve your goals. You can expect a promotion at work or recognition in school. You are also likely to get married now, or receive property, or be an honored guest.

Six at the top: The woman's basket is empty. The man stabs the sheep, but no blood comes. Nothing beneficial.

Do not expect to succeed in your enterprise. You may have a job but no salary, or recognition in school but no knowledge. Retired persons should watch out for declining health.

55. *Feng / Greatness*

The attributes of greatness, brilliance, and prosperity are suggested in several ways by this hexagram. *Chen*, the upper trigram, here means wood, forest, and thunder, while the lower trigram, *Li*, is fire, lightning, the sun, summer, and midday. Together they depict thunder and lightning, a forest in summer, or a forest ablaze, all scenes of great brilliance or power.

Chen, the eldest son, and *Li*, the middle daughter, also represent a couple in the prime of their marriage. They lead full, rich, happy lives, prosperous in business and active in society. But of course this state cannot last: age relentlessly advances and their energy declines, just as fire diminishes and the sun at midday begins its descent. All greatness changes into its opposite; this is a law of nature which cannot be avoided.

A person who receives this hexagram should be cautious of success and overabundance. A stockbroker whose business had been very successful received this hexagram, with a moving line in the sixth place, in 1970. I warned him to hold onto his assets and to handle his affairs judiciously. This he failed to do. When the stock market fell in 1971 his investments lost money, and his customers blamed him. Finally, he moved out of the city to avoid embarrassing contacts.

THE JUDGMENT
Greatness. Success.
The king attains greatness,
Without sadness; he should be like
The sun at midday.

THE SYMBOL
Thunder and lightning coming together
Symbolize Greatness.
The superior man judges lawsuits
And imposes punishments.

THE LINES
Nine at the bottom: When a man meets a deputy ruler, there will be harmony between them for ten days. No blame. Setting forth will lead to progress.

With the help of others you will achieve your goal. At work this may mean being promoted with the support of your supervisor; for school it indicates finishing a project and gaining recognition with the help of your friends. But if birth time and zodiac symbols are not favorable, you are liable to meet trouble.

Six in the second place: The shield is so great that you can see the polestar at noon. Undertakings will lead to suspicion and harm. Only truth can win the confidence of the ruler. Good fortune.

A person can expect to profit even under adverse conditions. A lawsuit will be cleared up without dispute, and patients will recover.

At work a person is liable to cause envy and slander, though his ideas are good; he will lose in the beginning but emerge vindicated. A person without a job will nevertheless find a chance to succeed.

If birth time and zodiac symbols are not favorable, one may mourn for his elders.

Nine in the third place: Heavy clouds—a fine drizzle can be seen. He hurts his right arm. No blame.

This line indicates that a person cannot achieve his goals. He may meet with slander, conflicts, or lawsuits, or have trouble in the hands and feet. At work one is apt to resign, and in school one will find it hard to improve.

Nine in the fourth place: The shield is so great that you can see the polestar at noon. One meets an ignorant ruler. Good fortune.

If you get this line, you should expect disharmony and instability at work; in school you will probably have a misunderstanding. Go to someone for advice. If you are in business, you can expect to travel and meet a new opportunity, but you should be cautious of accidents; do not go by ship.

Six in the fifth place: Glory will come, causing prosperity and recognition. Good fortune.

You can expect help from an influential person and success in your goal. An employed person will be respected in society, and a student will pass his exams and thus gain high recognition. Honor is in store for an older person.

Six at the top: One's house is big and luxurious; later it will be overgrown. Someone looks in at the gate and does not see anyone. For three years he sees nothing. Misfortune.

It is a time of conflict, gossip, and lawsuits. A person is likely to struggle with relatives, leave home, and start a career in another place. Even an important person is liable to encounter difficulty. The student, however, can expect to advance greatly.

56. *Lu / The Exile*

Lu indicates an exile or stranger, or traveling and wandering. *Li*, fire, burns on the mountain, *Ken*. The fire is fed by *Sun*, the lower nuclear trigram, which stands for the trees and grasses that grow on the mountain. *Sun* is also the wind which spreads the fire. The wind-blown fire and the fixed mountain symbolize the aimless wanderer and his place of exile. The upper nuclear trigram is *Tui*, the lake, and the waves blown by the wind on the lake also depict the state of transience.

This hexagram represents the situation in ancient times when traveling was difficult and arduous and those who traveled were usually friendless and lonely. Sometimes they would find shelter and friends (the second and fourth lines) but often there were troubles and misfortune (the third and sixth lines).

Lu is favorable for anyone who has to travel as part of his profession. It is unfavorable for marriage: both parties will change their minds, or if they are already married, they will be separated temporarily by their careers.

THE JUDGMENT
The Exile. Small success.
To continue leads to good fortune.

THE SYMBOL
Fire over the mountain
Symbolizes the Exile.
The superior man is careful and clever
In imposing punishments, and does not delay
The cases brought.

THE LINES
Six at the bottom: If the exile dallies with petty matters,
he will draw disaster on himself.

Narrow-mindedness will cause misfortune. One lacks ability in
his job. If one is meek in school, he will be insulted.

Six in the second place: The exile arrives at an inn. He
carries valuables. He wins the loyalty of a young servant.

This line indicates that a person will be successful in a remote
location. At work one can expect an important job or an assignment involving some aspect of the military; a student will achieve
recognition and a job offer.

This is a good time to repair one's home or get assistance in work.

Nine in the third place: The inn where the exile stays
burns down. He loses the loyalty of his young servant. To
continue is dangerous.

If you get this line, you should be prepared for trouble in family
affairs. At work you are in danger of losing your job, and in school,
your reputation. Be especially vigilant against fires in your home.

Nine in the fourth place: The exile finds rest in a sanctuary.
He regains his valuables. He is not happy in his heart.

A person is likely to succeed somewhere away from his home.
Perhaps one will receive a promotion to a branch of the company in

another city or join the military. But if birth time and zodiac symbols are not favorable, there may be sadness, mourning, and injury.

Six in the fifth place: He shoots a pheasant, losing one arrow. In the end he gains honor and position.

Expect great success. Those employed will have responsibility and prestige; students and scholars will pass their exams, get jobs, and gain recognition; and women will find satisfying careers.

Nine at the top: A bird's nest burns. The exile laughs in the beginning, laments later. He loses his cow by being careless. Misfortune.

One should live cautiously to avoid the misfortune which arises from good fortune. A person will be honored in the beginning, but he is liable to lose his high position later.

This is also a time when one can expect to move or repair his home. He should watch out for trouble in his eyes and be careful with electrical appliances and fire.

57. *Sun / Penetration (Wind)*

Both the upper and lower trigrams are *Sun*: wind, wood, and penetration. Trees and grasses bend before the wind, just as the people yield to the directives of their governments. Those who receive this hexagram should be flexible and work harmoniously with others. Even if one lacks money or skill, he can still achieve success by following someone great. But do not follow another blindly: a definite goal is necessary for good fortune.

The wind, *Sun*, scatters the seeds of plants to the ends of the earth. Eventually they fall to the ground, penetrate the soil, and begin to grow. After the new plants bloom, seeds are once again produced and the process is repeated, generation after generation. Thus this hexagram indicates that people can become prosperous in another land. It is favorable for those in the travel business and those who travel for a living.

Years ago, one of my countrymen, who couldn't make up his mind whether or not to go to America, received this hexagram with a changing line in the fifth place. I told him that although his going to America would turn out favorably, he would experience difficulty at first; after six years he would achieve success. He did go and opened a Chinese restaurant. The first three years were difficult owing to lack of money, but each year the restaurant prospered more and more. After six years he not only became successful but he also married a cashier who worked in the restaurant, and they have subsequently raised children.

THE JUDGMENT
Penetration. Small success.
It is beneficial to go somewhere.
It is beneficial to see a great man.

THE SYMBOL
Wind following wind
Symbolizes Penetration.
The superior man proclaims his directives
And executes his affairs.

THE LINES
Six at the bottom: Advance and retreat. It benefits the military person to be firm.

People will both gain and lose in their enterprises. Those employed will have to cope with instability in their jobs: they may be either promoted or demoted, or perhaps they will hold two jobs. But after a difficult situation they will gain success. A student will be wise to seek a civil service job. The time is not favorable for a military position.

Nine in the second place: Wind under the bed. Many fortunetellers and witches are used. Good fortune. No blame.

You will succeed through honesty. If employed you will be promoted (you may find a job involving either speech or writing); if a student you can expect recognition. You may also take part in a religious ceremony.

Nine in the third place: Orders repeated many times. Humiliation.

Sudden gain, sudden loss. Working people will be demoted or dismissed, or they may travel on business. It is a time of embarrassment and humiliation.

Six in the fourth place: Remorse disappears. One catches three kinds of game while hunting.

Benefits and good fortune are in store for many. A person may get a job in a remote place or receive an important assignment having to do with the military. Students can look forward to recognition.

Nine in the fifth place: Firmness—good fortune. Remorse disappears. Everything is of benefit. Loss in the beginning, gain in the end. Three days before change. Three days after change. Good fortune.

A person will benefit from his situation and have good fortune. Even with a promotion the employed person faces obstacles in the beginning, but success will come later; he may have two jobs or a powerful position. Recognition is in store for the academic.

Nine at the top: Wind under the bed. He loses his wealth. Continuing leads to misfortune.

This line indicates possible loss or sickness. At work you should be wary of losing your job, and in school you should avoid showing arrogance. But if birth time and zodiac symbols are favorable, there will be success; good fortune will arise from bad.

58. *Tui / Joyousness*

The essence of *Tui* is joyousness, happiness, and beauty; it implies success. Both primary trigrams are *Tui*: the youngest daughter, joyous, and the lake. Two lakes in the same hexagram emphasize the beneficial aspects of a lake, for human beings and plant and animal life, for navigation and irrigation, and for the enhancement of the scenery. The person who receives this hexagram will achieve success or receive benefits.

The trigram *Tui* represents the mouth. The hexagram therefore indicates a career involving speaking. You may become a singer, actor or actress, teacher, commentator, or diplomat. You should beware, however, for excessive talking can lead to trouble.

For business this hexagram means success. *Tui* is gold, and the double trigram means a great deal of it; in addition, *Tui* refers to autumn, when fruits and vegetables ripen and nature is ready for the harvest. In love affairs, the hexagram indicates that two women will love one man, and for married couples the two mouths mean constant disputes.

THE JUDGMENT

Joyousness. Success.
Continuance is favorable.

THE SYMBOL

The beautiful lakes
Symbolize Joyousness.
The superior man joins his fellows
For teaching and study.

THE LINES

Nine at the bottom: Harmonious joyousness. Good fortune.

This is a time of harmony. A person can expect benefit, recognition, success, and an important job. Husbands and wives will get along well. But if birth time and zodiac symbols are not favorable, one may suffer conflicts and lawsuits.

Nine in the second place: Truthful joyousness. Good fortune. Remorse vanishes.

A person who gets this line will increase his proficiency and be in harmony with others; he can expect a promotion, or, if still in school, a good opportunity. Even if his affairs are now tangled, he will free himself.

Six in the third place: Coming joyousness. Misfortune.

Do not follow another blindly, or mistakes and danger will result. Flattery at work will be viewed as misconduct. In school you can expect to be involved in a competitive situation.

Nine in the fourth place: Considering joyousness does not bring serenity. Once one corrects his conduct, one has joyousness.

This is a time when merchants will benefit, patients will improve, and students will have the chance to advance. At work one can expect added responsibility and the chance for promotion. But he should be careful to avoid evildoers. Many will enlarge their families through marriage or having children. But peace of mind will be elusive now.

Nine in the fifth place: Confidence in what is decaying is dangerous.

If you get this line, you should expect trouble caused by an unworthy person. At work beware of slander. If in school, you may be held back.

Six at the top: Enticing joyousness.

Although people can count on the help or recommendations of others, they will still not be able to achieve their goals or gain the recognition they seek. One should expect trouble—perhaps in the eyes—and gossip.

59. *Huan / Dispersion*

This hexagram means dispersion, dissolution, and separation. Dispersion is symbolized by the wind (*Sun*, the upper trigram) blowing the water (*K'an*, the lower), causing waves, spray, and mist. *Sun* also means wood, thus the trigrams represent boats on the water as well.

Boats on the water imply traveling, and the Judgment says, "It is of benefit to cross the great water." It would be good for you to travel to another place for an undertaking, but in a more general sense the hexagram advises that it is time for a change or movement of some kind. Move your home, alter your attitude or ideas, change your career, begin a new venture, or open a new branch of your business. With the changed conditions, misfortune will dissolve into good fortune. It is also a good time for religious and political activities. Sick people will recover.

Although this hexagram augurs good conditions—none of the lines is misfortune—it advises care. As with sailing a boat at sea, you must be on the watch constantly for dangerous conditions. Something may be broken up: a separation in the family or a dispersion of property. For people interested in marriage, this hexagram implies that both parties will be busy with their work; they will not have the time or opportunity to get married.

THE JUDGMENT
Dispersion. Success.
The king approaches the temple.
It is of benefit to cross the great water.
It benefits to continue.

THE SYMBOL
Wind blowing over water

Symbolizes Dispersion.
The ancient kings offered sacrifices
To the Deity, then built temples.

THE LINES
Six at the bottom: To rescue one with a strong horse.
Good fortune.

The first line indicates the approval of your superiors. A student will advance because of his projects, and a workingman can expect promotion.

Nine in the second place: At the dispersion he hastens to the opportunity. Remorse vanishes.

This is a time when people achieve their goals and fulfill their wishes. Perhaps one will get married and have a family. At work a person can expect to gain power, perhaps even rising to the top of his company. But if birth time and zodiac symbols are not favorable, one may lose something or be forced to move.

Six in the third place: He dissolves his egotism. No remorse.

A person should be wary of disaster: if it occurs, he may not be able to escape its results.

During this time a person is likely to be transferred in his job to another location. A student can complete his studies somewhere else, but he still will not get a job. In any case it is not a good time for him to begin a new undertaking.

Six in the fourth place: He disperses his group. Great and fortune. He disperses his hills (property). Ordinary people do not think of this.

Danger in the beginning but safety later. One can expect to achieve his goals and make a profit. At work one is likely to become the leader of many; in school one will pass his exams and gain recognition. But if birth time and zodiac symbols are not favorable, a time of mourning may be in store.

Nine in the fifth place: Dispersion is like sweat pouring

from the body, with loud cries. Separation from the king's palace. No blame.

If you get this line, you can expect benefit and protection from danger. You will find a job, or, if you already have one, a promotion is likely. If in school, you will complete your courses and be recognized.

Nine at the top: Dissolving his (coagulated) blood. Departing to a remote place. No blame.

Now is the time to retreat from dangerous situations. Sick people can expect relief, and a lawsuit will be decided favorably. If a person is working, he is apt to be transferred to another place, or he may find a job with the military. Students will have the chance to work for the good of society.

If birth time and zodiac symbols are not favorable, one should expect trouble with blood circulation.

60. *Chieh / Limitation*

Limitation implies both control and thrift. *K'an*, the upper trigram, means water and danger. The lower trigram is *Tui*, the lake and joyousness. Unless there are boundaries to limit the water in the lake and ways to measure it, there will be flooding. Applied to personal affairs this means that when one is happy and joyous, he should still beware of danger and thus not lose control.

Limitation also means coming to a stop. *Chen*, movement and strength, is the lower nuclear trigram, while the upper nuclear trigram is *Ken*, keeping still. Even though strong, one should check his actions in order to avoid danger, *K'an*.

The person who receives this hexagram should follow the middle way between extremes and keep a good sense of proportion. The first line advocates not leaving one's resting place; the second line cautions against staying. The fourth and fifth lines suggest that limitation at the proper level can be sweet, while the top line means that overdoing it produces bitterness. One should not go hungry, but neither should he overeat. In business, limitation means avoiding large expenses while at the same time not being overly hesitant when faced with opportunities for growth.

THE JUDGMENT
Limitation. Success.
Bitter limitation should not be continued.

THE SYMBOL
Water above the lake
Symbolizes Limitation.
The superior man devises number and measure,
And measures conduct and virtue.

THE LINES
Nine at the bottom: One does not go out of the door and courtyard. No blame.

The first line suggests that one should keep his present career and live in the same place without loss. If a person is in school, he will not find the opportunity he is seeking now; he should wait for a proper chance.

If birth time and zodiac symbols are not favorable, one is likely to meet danger.

Nine in the second place: One does not go out the gate and courtyard. Misfortune.

Generally, this line bodes good fortune for action and misfortune for inaction. Ignorance of the current situation will lead to the loss of an opportunity because one did not undertake anything or did not leave home; at work one may lose a chance for promotion. At this time recommendations will provide no help for the student.

Six in the third place: One does not limit oneself and has cause for lamenting. No blame.

This line implies that you have heavy expenses and cannot handle money well: you are probably living too luxuriously. If you are in school, you may be unable to maintain your position because of harsh attacks against you.

Six in the fourth place: Peaceful limitation. Success.

If you follow regulations you can expect good fortune and recognition. At work you are likely to achieve your career goals through the favor of a superior.

Nine in the fifth place: Sweet limitation. Good fortune. Undertakings bring honor.

A person who gets this line can expect to have his way. At work he will be promoted; if out of work or in school, he will find a job.

Six at the top: Bitter limitation. Continuing brings misfortune. Remorse vanishes.

If you lose control you will be blamed for it, if you insist on your ideas at work you will be humiliated, if you lack self-confidence in school you will suffer remorse. And if birth time and zodiac symbols are not favorable, you will gain neither money nor recognition.

And old man should be careful of his health.

61. *Chung Fu / Inner Truthfulness*

Chung Fu indicates sincerity, truthfulness, and confidence; it also signifies someone who possesses these qualities and is trusted by others. The upper trigram is *Sun,* the eldest daughter and gentleness; the lower is *Tui*, the youngest daughter and joyousness. The older girl treats her little sister gently and with kindliness, and the younger girl follows happily; in business this kind of relationship results in harmony between employer and employee. *Ken* and *Chen*, the nuclear trigrams, are the youngest and the eldest son, respectively. Thus the entire hexagram consists of brothers and sisters who are able to help and rely on each other.

Chung Fu presages good fortune: harmony in society, cooperation with family and friends, and success in undertakings. The eldest daughter and youngest son, youngest daughter and eldest son are balanced in their relationship. In shape the hexagram resembles a kiss between lovers. It also augurs a change in one's location: the Judgment says, "It is of benefit to cross the great water." The time is also good for marriages or love affairs.

But one should show caution: good fortune does not last forever. In the top line, to continue means misfortune. Too much confidence and celebration can be harmful.

THE JUDGMENT
Inner Truthfulness. Sea lions—good fortune.
It is of benefit to cross the great water.
To continue brings benefit.

THE SYMBOL
The wind over the lake
Symbolizes Inner Truthfulness.
The superior man judges criminals
And postpones capital punishment.

THE LINES
Nine at the bottom: Ponder carefully. Good fortune.
Other thoughts lead to anxiety.

Aided by an influential person, you will be able to achieve your goal. You should work hard to succeed, however, for sadness will hide in happiness and there may be loss: laziness will lead ultimately to failure.

A working person can expect a promotion through a recommendation, and for a student this is a good time for an undertaking.

Nine in the second place: A crane calls in the shade; its young ones respond. I have a good goblet (wine, virtue) to share with you.

Benefit everywhere. People will have children, receive benefits, or live long lives. Those employed will be promoted, and the unemployed will find jobs. But old people may become ill.

Six in the third place: One meets a person. Suddenly he beats a drum, and suddenly he stops; then he weeps, then he sings.

You can expect to gain sometimes, but also to lose sometimes; in happiness hides sadness, but from sadness will spring joy. Working people may be promoted now, but demoted later.

Six in the fourth place: The moon will be full. He loses a team of horses. No blame.

If you get this line, you can expect a recommendation from your supervisor at work followed by a promotion. If you are in school, you will complete your courses and gain recognition.

If birth time and zodiac symbols are unfavorable, a married person may lose his spouse.

Nine in the fifth place: His truthfulness is steadfast. No blame.

Good fortune in everything. People will be in harmony with society and achieve their goals. Those employed will get along with their associates and receive added responsibility, while students will have a chance for advancement and recognition.

Nine at the top: The crow of a cock piercing the heavens. To continue—misfortune.

Nine at the top foretells that a person will compete with a stranger and become involved in entanglements that are difficult to escape. At work the employee will have the chance to associate with a high official; in school the student can expect a great advance.

If birth time and zodiac symbols are unfavorable, however, one will have poor health.

62. *Hsiao Kuo / Slight Excess*

Hsiao Kuo signifies the slight excess or small mistake that can prevent the achievement of great things. *Chen,* the upper trigram, the eldest son and thunder, is characterized by strength and movement. *Ken,* the youngest son and mountain, the lower trigram, is characterized by strength and stillness. There is an excess of strength in this situation, but it cannot be exerted because of the opposing tendencies of movement and stillness.

Applied to human affairs, the hexagram indicates excessive humbleness, stinginess, and lack of purpose. A person with these qualities cannot carry out schemes on a grand scale because he is not willing to chance great success. Thus he loses opportunities and finds it difficult to advance in society; he may even bring harm on himself. This kind of person must either change his attitude and become both more generous and more purposeful or settle for only small achievements.

The preceding hexagram, *Chung Fu,* portrays two people mouth-to-mouth; in *Hsiao Kuo* they are back-to-back, meaning that there is no harmony. One should be cautious constantly: the third line says that someone will strike from behind.

THE JUDGMENT

Slight Excess. Success.
Continuing is of benefit.
Undertaking small things, not great things.
The song of the flying bird.
It is not good to go up;
It is good to stay below.
Great good fortune.

THE SYMBOL

Thunder over the mountain
Symbolizes Slight Excess.
The superior man's conduct is overly humble;
In mourning he laments exceedingly,
And he is stingy in his spending.

THE LINES

Six at the bottom: A bird encounters misfortune when it soars.

If you get this line, you can expect good fortune at first, but misfortune may strike later. Perhaps you will be rapidly promoted at work, but this will cause trouble. If you are in school, you can expect to pass your exams and receive high recognition.

Six in the second place: He passes over his deceased grandfather and meets his deceased grandmother. He does not reach the king but meets an official. No blame.

This line indicates help from both a woman and an influential person; one can expect to achieve his goals, get a promotion, and make profits. A student will now be successful in an undertaking and have a good teacher.

But if birth time and zodiac symbols are not favorable, one's mother is liable to suffer ill health.

Nine in the third place: If he does not protect himself carefully, someone will stab him in the back. Misfortune.

Be very cautious at this time: beware of harm caused by a woman or by people whose evil is hidden.

Nine in the fourth place: He meets things without excessive reactions. No blame. He will meet danger if he advances. There must be caution. Do not continue.

You can expect to maintain your present job or position without harm or setback. For a student, this is a time of fine opportunity: he will pass his exams easily.

Six in the fifth place: Heavy clouds come from the west, but no rain. What the duke shoots he takes from its cave.

This line indicates a favorable time to keep your present position without undertaking anything new or great, although the employed person should perhaps consider a vacation. A student should expect poor conditions, but he will be aided by an influential person. The aged and sick should beware of misfortune.

Six at the top: He passes over someone, not meeting him. The birds fly away. Misfortune. There will be disaster.

According to this line you will tend to be ambitious beyond your position and capacity; at work your arrogance will cause frustration. If you are a student, however, you can expect to finish a research project successfully.

If birth time and zodiac symbols are not favorable, however, there is likely to be mourning.

63. *Chi Chi / Completion*

Chi Chi means something achieved successfully, completed, or accomplished, like studies for a degree. The primary trigrams, *Li* below and *K'an* above, depict useful technology in action: the fire boils the water, producing steam. There is an equal and proper distribution of yin and yang lines—unbroken lines in strong positions, broken lines in yielding positions—which indicates balance and harmony in all things. In nature this state of perfection is demonstrated by the full moon or by a flower in bloom; in life by a young man and young woman living together harmoniously. But the full moon must wane and the flower fade: people who are successful may easily decline.

According to the Judgment, the hexagram predicts success for small undertakings. In business affairs it means that you should not expand but maintain the present state of your business. For marriages it denotes peace and harmony; lovers should get married quickly, without delay.

For your undertaking the Judgment also indicates good fortune in the beginning, but disorder in the end. Here is an example: in 1945, during the Sino-Japanese War, when I made a prediction for the Nationalist Chinese forces, I received Hexagram 36, *Ming I*, with the moving line in the fifth position; the hexagram therefore changed to *Chi Chi*. The Nationalists did become victorious over the Japanese. Two years later, however, disorder broke out in the form of civil war, and eventually the Nationalists were defeated by the Communists and lost control of mainland China.

THE JUDGMENT
Completion. Success in the small.
It benefits to continue.
Good fortune at first; disorder in the end.

THE SYMBOL
Water above fire symbolizes Completion.
The superior man ponders danger
And takes precautions against it.

THE LINES
Nine at the bottom: The brake to the wheel. The tail gets wet. No blame.

Caution prevents trouble. A person has the wish to begin an enterprise but he will not; he will begin something else but not complete it for a time. If one has a job, he will receive no salary in the beginning. A student will not be able to find a job.

Six in the second place: A lady loses her carriage curtain. Without seeking it, it will be regained within seven days.

You will experience difficulty, trouble, and loss in the beginning, but you will be successful later. If birth time and zodiac symbols are not favorable, however, you should beware of poor health.

Nine in the third place: The emperor Kao Tsung chastised the barbarian country and conquered it in three years. The inferior man should no longer be employed.

People should expect many troubles: conflicts, lawsuits, and jealousies will all cost them money. But with patience and perseverance, students and the unemployed will find jobs. A person already working is likely to take a business trip or be called to work outside the city where he now lives.

Six in the fourth place: One has silk clothes but wears rags. Be cautious all day.

This line indicates that you can expect to have enough money to live comfortably. If you are without a job or are a student, your knowledge and ability will lead to success in an undertaking. If you are now working, you can safely keep your position by taking precautions.

At this time travel cautiously; there could be trouble with transportation.

Nine in the fifth place: The eastern neighbor sacrificed an ox; the western neighbor made a simple offering, but he received the blessing.

Many will succeed in small undertakings but fail in grand schemes. Those employed will hold high positions either in society or in religion, but others will be jealous of them. Students and the unemployed are liable to see their opportunities vanish. An undertaking in the west will bring good fortune, in the east misfortune.

Six at the top: His head gets wet. Danger.

Avoid evil persons lest you yourself become tainted. At work a person with responsibilities may be subject to jealousy and danger. Students and the unemployed should not neglect their opportunities.

Caution in traveling is advised now.

64. *Wei Chi / Before Completion*

Although *Wei Chi* is the last hexagram of the *I Ching*, it signifies a time of great effort or concentration just before something is completed. In structure and meaning it is the opposite of the preceding hexagram, *Chi Chi.* In *Wei Chi* the unbroken (yang) lines are in yielding positions, while the broken (yin) lines are in strong positions. *Li*, fire or sun, is above *K'an*, water; the image they present is that of the sun rising from the sea at dawn. Everything is about to begin, and you should be prepared. Or perhaps there is an unfinished project or some business that you should work on diligently.

Even though completion or success is not yet at hand, this hexagram contains great hope for the future. In business this is the time for a fresh undertaking; new investments will yield profits. If you are a student or scholar, choose your subject or field of research carefully, otherwise you will waste your time. In marriage, the position of the lines indicates that the husband should yield to the wife. The trigrams also show this: the female, *Li*, is above, the male, *K'an*, below.

In 1970 *Wei Chi* appeared on my astrological chart, with the moving line in the fourth position. Soon afterward, in February of that same year, I lectured in New Hampshire, and a favorable article about my presentation appeared in a Boston Sunday newspaper. These were the events before completion. In 1972 my book *T'ai Chi Ch'uan and I Ching* was published and I was invited to appear on television in Boston. Thus the prophecy of the fourth line was fulfilled: "Within three years, rewards from the Great Country."

THE JUDGMENT

Before Completion. Success.
A young fox almost across

Wets his tail in the water.
Nothing benefits.

THE SYMBOL
Fire above water
Symbolizes Before Completion.
The superior man carefully distinguishes things,
And puts them in their appropriate place.

THE LINES
Six at the bottom: He wets his tail. Humiliation.

One cannot achieve his goal. Employed people will meet with obstacles and find the situation difficult to improve. Students will pass their exams, but their standing will still be low and they will achieve only small success. The traveler should be cautious.

Nine in the second place: He brakes the wheel.
Continuing—good fortune.

By keeping your original attitude, you can complete your plans, but acting roughly will lead to trouble. At your job you should work hard and win the confidence of others. Students and the unemployed, however, should not expect to find jobs now.

Six in the third place: Before completion (achieving success), continuing—misfortune. It is beneficial to cross the great water.

This line indicates frustration. In school the student will show no progress, but at work the employee's adequate ability will make it easy for him to cooperate with others. Merchants may profit now from business trips.

The time is not favorable for climbing or crossing high mountains.

Nine in the fourth place: Continuing—good fortune. Remorse vanishes. Great power is used to attack the land of the barbarians. Within three years, rewards from the Great Country.

You are likely to profit with the help of others. Responsibility and success are in store for an employed person, or perhaps he will accept a military position. The academic's examinations lead to honors.

Six in the fifth place: Continuing—good fortune. No remorse. The glory of the superior man wins the confidence of the people. Good fortune.

Many will be successful in their activities and become wealthy. Those employed will get high promotions, and a student will gain recognition through his writings.

Nine at the top: He drinks wine with confidence. No blame. When his head gets wet, he loses confidence.

A person who receives this line will be able to escape danger. An older person will enjoy his life, but he should beware of misfortune in the form of drunkenness or drowning. At work one can expect to advance to an important job.

Yarrow Stalks for Prediction

Symbol and Number

Of the two systems of Chinese prediction, symbolic and numerical, the symbolic is older, dating back to the use of tortoise shells.
People in ancient times exposed the shells to fire until one of three
different patterns of cracks appeared: one looked like broken jade,
another like roof tiles, and the third resembled the cracks in dry
land. From these the predictors learned of good fortune and misfortune in the future. But the method they used is not mentioned
in the *I Ching* and is now lost to us, probably in the great book
burning of the third century B.C.

The *I Ching* does mention yarrow stalks—the ancient numerical
method of prediction—and people who consult the Book of Changes
still use this method to determine the correct hexagram. Yarrow is
a perennial herb that grows in north-temperate regions. Some years
ago a national magazine showed a man predicting with a bunch of
grass stems which he threw to the ground, obviously unaware of the
proper method. An article in a major metropolitan newspaper told
of a person who used spaghetti sticks instead of yarrow stalks. Many
Chinese people use chopsticks as a substitute. In this chapter the
proper yarrow stalk method is explained.

The Chinese character for yarrow stalks, *Ch'i*, has three parts: the
top part means "grass," the middle means "old," and the bottom
means "the sun." Without the grass part, the character means "old
man," a respected figure in China. All this indicates that the yarrow
stalks were not considered common grass; rather, they were allowed
to grow for a period of years to gain their spiritual nourishment,
just as people must live many years to acquire knowledge and experience. In the *Ta Chuan* it is written: "Therefore: Heaven creates

divine things; the holy sage takes them as models." To gain this
divine nature a long growth was needed, so the stalks could provide
good service between the people and the *I Ching.*

Yarrow stalks that were employed especially for prediction had
another name, *Shih.* In this character the top part is bamboo and
the bottom is a witch, which indicates that already in ancient times
bamboo was used as a subsitute for yarrow stalks. Bamboo was readily
available, while well-aged yarrow stalks were hard to find.

How to Use Yarrow Stalks

In your approach to the *I Ching,* you should begin by praying,
the same way as when using the coin method; in your prayer say
who you are, where you live, and what your question is. Then light
incense and pass the yarrow stalks through the smoke, all the time
concentrating on your question.

You must start with a bunch of fifty yarrow stalks, although only
forty-nine are actually used. From the fifty take one and put it aside;
it is not used again. On a flat surface in front of you, separate the
forty-nine stalks at random into two groups. From the pile on the
right take out one stalk with your right hand and put it between the
ring finger and little finger of your left hand. (Throughout the process
the right hand does the counting, separating, and picking up, while
the left hand does the holding.) Now with your right hand count
through the left bunch of stalks by fours until there is a remainder of
just one, two, three, or four stalks. Put this remainder between the
ring and middle fingers of your left hand. Then count through the
bunch of stalks on the right in the same way and put that remainder
between the middle and index fingers of the left hand. Count the
total number of stalks you are now holding in your left hand. It will
be either five or nine. Write this number down, put these stalks
aside, and then put the two groups of remaining stalks together
again. Now repeat the process: separate the stalks at random, take
one from the right, put it between the little and ring fingers, and
proceed to count through the two bunches by fours as before, first
left and then right, putting the remainders in the left hand. This
time you will have a total of four or eight stalks. Write this number
down, put these stalks aside, and repeat the process one more time
with the stalks that remain. Again the total of stalks in your left

hand will be either four or eight. These three processes complete the manipulations necessary to arrive at the bottom line of the hexa-gram.

You can now compute what the bottom line is. Of the totals obtained, nine and eight are considered to have the same significance and both are assigned the number two; five and four are also considered of equal significance and are assigned the number three. Therefore you will have, after changing the three separate totals to their assigned numbers and adding them, a new total of six, seven, eight, or nine. Six is Old Yin—a changing broken line; seven is Young Yang—as unchanging unbroken line; eight is Young Yin—an unchanging broken line; nine is Old Yang—a changing unbroken line.

Repeat this series of manipulations five times to obtain the other five lines of the hexagram.

Numerology

The numerical system of prediction later developed into a system of numerology. Over two thousand years after the *I Ching* was written, the great Chinese mathematician-philosopher Shao Yung (A.D. 1011–1078) devised the Plum Blossom Numerology, which contains various formulas for prediction based on number. The formulas involve not only the text of the *I Ching,* but also the interaction of the Five Elements, the conditions at the moment of prediction, and the date. Unlike the coin and yarrow-stalk methods, Shao Yung's numerology requires no instrument of prediction, and there is only one moving line for each hexagram obtained. Once the formulas and symbolism have been memorized, a prediction can be made in less than a minute. I myself have used the formulas from the Plum Blossom Numerology and am always amazed at their accuracy.

The Trigrams and Their Attributes

Trigram	Symbol	Characteristics	Family Relationship	Animal	Body Part	Time, Season
Ch'ien ☰	Heaven	Creative Strong Light Yang	Father	Horse	Head	Late Autumn–Early Winter
K'un ☷	Earth	Receptive Devoted Yielding Dark Yin	Mother	Cow Mare	Belly	Late Summer–Early Autumn
Chen ☳	Thunder	Arousing Moving Excited Strong	Eldest Son	Galloping Horse Dragon	Foot	Spring
K'an ☵	Water	Dangerous Abysmal Cunning	Middle Son	Pig	Ear	Winter

Ken ☶	Mountain	Keeping Still Quiet Stubborn	Youngest Son	Dog Rat	Hand Finger	Late Winter– Early Spring
Sun ☴	Wind (also Wood)	Penetrating Gentle Undecided Yielding	Eldest Daughter	Cock	Thigh Upperarm	Late Spring– Early Summer
Li ☲	Fire (also Sun, Lightning)	Clinging Light-giving Hot Beautiful Agitated	Middle Daughter	Pheasant Shellfish	Eye	Summer
Tui ☱	Lake	Joyous Laughing Soft Gossipy	Youngest Daughter	Sheep	Mouth	Autumn

Chart for Identifying the Hexagrams

TRIGRAMS Upper / Lower	Ch'ien	Chen	K'an	Ken	K'un	Sun	Li	Tui
Ch'ien	1	34	5	26	11	9	14	43
Chen	25	51	3	27	24	42	21	17
K'an	6	40	29	4	7	59	64	47
Ken	33	62	39	52	15	53	56	31
K'un	12	16	8	23	2	20	35	45
Sun	44	32	48	18	46	57	50	28
Li	13	55	63	22	36	37	30	49
Tui	10	54	60	41	19	61	38	58

74 75 76 77 10 9 8 7 6 5 4 3 2 1